*T*WO

Two

THE NEW AMERICAN RELIGION

*A summary publication in the nineteenth year
of the first nineteen-year cycle*

Anonymous

Writer's Showcase presented by *Writer's Digest*
San Jose New York Lincoln Shanghai

Two
The New American Religion

Published by Writer's Showcase presented by *Writer's Digest*
an imprint of iUniverse.com, Inc.

For information address:
iUniverse.com, Inc.
620 North 48th Street
Suite 201
Lincoln, NE 68504-3467
www.iuniverse.com

ISBN: 0-595-09534-8

Printed in the United States of America

Epigraph

Sending messages back and forth to the spiritual realms seems to be a native human activity; through these messages, life is made easier and less lonely, beauty brought forth along with fairness and moral quality. For all these things, human beings are pregnant when they have been filled from contact with the Two Sources. Life in contact with the Two Sources allows people to communicate with their first and final states. From *them* we come and to *them* we will return; in between those two events, it is possible to comprehend the enormity of how males and females came to be.

An excerpt from Chapter 2, Who We Are: The Basic Philosophy, "The American Psyche"

Contents

Foreword

Two is a new religion that began to form in Ann Arbor, Michigan, in 1982. For the first 15 years it was a developing spiritual philosophy. In 1997 work began to convert the philosophy into a framework for a new religion, an American religion. The result of that work is this book. It is hoped that this public document will act as a catalyst to continue the process of forming this new religion and expand the membership from a few to many.

The *Two* religion is based on American culture, American heritage, and American values. *Two* is, in many ways, very different from the Arab-based religions (such as Christianity, Judaism, and Islam); East Indian practices (such as Hinduism and Buddhism); and the Asian philosophical and religious systems (such as Taoism and Confucianism). *Two* is a religion that assumes there are two basic creative Sources: one that is responsible for the idea of a male and another that is responsible for the idea of a female. Working together, these Two Sources create from themselves all of the various kinds of males and females on earth. Male and female human beings can send messages to and receive messages from the Two Sources through the use of the "quiet voice" inside their head and through the "gut feelings" near the pit of their stomach. These messages are referred to as "spiritual messages." The basic function of the *Two* religion is to help a person learn to send and receive spiritual messages as clearly as possible. *Two*, by its very American nature, is a more personal, privately centered and much less public religion, focused entirely upon spiritual matters.

Over the past nineteen years and through the use of yearly manuscripts, a relatively small group of people endeavored to understand how to produce the clearest possible spiritual messages. An individual human life appears to be more pleasant and much easier if spiritual messages can be clearly understood. Life is more pleasant because life seems less lonely when one is in contact with the Two Sources. Life is easier because a person can learn how to "be at the right place at the right time." The task ahead is to gradually refine the understanding of how to clarify spiritual messages and share that information with people who express an interest in *Two*.

For the immediate future, *Two* is intended to function under certain "preferred practices." These practices are intended to help ensure that the religion remains focused only upon helping an individual person send and receive spiritual messages for the purpose of determining personal behavior (realizing that personal behavior must also conform to the laws and traditions of the United States of America). The preferred practices are also intended to prevent the religion from developing into a personality cult; from owning religious property; from becoming a large, centralized organization; from collecting money; and from other religious practices common to the Old World religions.

There seems to be no need for priests, ministers, rabbis, bishops, or popes—likewise no need for prophets, saints, or mystical people. Ordinary people seem perfectly capable of discovering what needs to be discovered. Information about the religion can easily be disseminated by what we call the "modern oral tradition"—one-to-one communication supplemented by the worldwide Web and by electronic mail. It is hoped that the modern oral tradition will become the preferred method for dissemination and refinement of the religion because each time the story is told it can be slightly modified to suit the teller and the listener. The religion, thereby, should have no fixed spiritual ideology beyond a basic framework and should remain dynamic and always changing.

There are no sacred written books for the religion. The intention, at the moment, is to limit written material to summary publications authored anonymously and made available to the general public only every nineteen years (see Preferred Practice # 9). This book is one such summary publication and as such is nothing more than a chronicle of the fundamental ideas and preferred practices of the religion as they exist at this point in time.

Additional information is available at our Web site:
www.NewAmericanReligion.org

Questions or general email may be addressed to:
Two@NewAmericanReligion.org

List of Contributors

Each year for the past nineteen years, 1982-2000, a manuscript (see Chronology of Manuscripts) was prepared by one person, a self-designated technical support person, documenting the philosophy to date. Each year around the time of the autumnal equinox, the manuscript was formally concluded and edited.

After editing, the editor's changes were incorporated into the manuscript. The manuscript was photocopied and bound. Three to five different people were asked to read the manuscript and write comments in the margins. Sometimes a reader would make comments for several consecutive years in a row. Mostly, however, new readers were chosen each year based solely on their interest in being a reader. After all the readers had completed their comments, the manuscripts were returned to the technical support person. The technical support person used the reader's comments along with other refinements to begin to revise the manuscript for the next year.

This yearly revision cycle went on each year of the first nineteen-year cycle. There were thirty-five to fifty different readers for this particular book. Special thanks go out to each reader and editor for their participation. A very warm thank you goes out to the primary editor for her work during the early years. We are not allowed to mention these people by name (Preferred Practice #9), although each person knows what he or she did and each person deserves our special thanks.

Two historical notes: (1) The religion, as such, did not begin to form and was not called *Two* until about year sixteen of the first nineteen-year cycle, and (2) Two yearly manuscripts, both poems, exist from the period 1979-1981 and are considered background manuscripts.

Chronology of Manuscripts

Background Manuscripts
1979-1981   *Song of Life.*
             Upon the Nature of: Our Universe Rhythm.

The Nineteen-Year Cycle Manuscripts
Year 1 1982 *A Twelve-Part Essay About: The Both of You and Me.*
Year 2 1983 *The One and The Other (A Model).*
Year 3 1984 *The One and The Other: A Model To Portray The Dual Nature of Awareness.*
Year 4 1985 *The One and The Other. A Model To Portray: Our Solar System, Some Atoms, The Formation and Movement of Earth, The Source of Female, The Source of Male, Contact With Those Sources, and Names For Those Sources.*
Year 5 1986 *An Imaginary Model To Portray The Origin of Male, The Origin of Female and Related Discussions.*
Year 6 1987 *The Both of You and Us. An ancient essay revised for modern times to create an imaginary model to portray the two basic forces of our Solar System.*

Year 7 1988 *A Discussion In Three Sections About The Two Basic Forces of Our Solar System and Males and Females on Earth.*

Year 8 1989 *The Two Basic Forces of Our Solar System and Males and Females On Earth.*

Year 9 1990 *The Book of Two.*

Year 10 1991 Four manuscripts were printed.

The Book of Two.

The Book of Two. A Poem.

The Book of Two. Five Poems.

A Declaration of Two.

Year 11 1992 No manuscripts dated 1992.

Year 12 1993 Two manuscripts were printed.

A Book About You and Me. By Me.

A Book About Us. By Us.

Year 13 1994 *About the Natures of Our Environment: What Am I Made From? How Did I Get Here? Who Am I? What Is My Relationship to the Environment? What Can I Expect When I Die?*

Year 14 1995 *The Quartet: Light, Matter, Male, Female.*

Year 15 1996 *A Report from The Designated Driver (getting from the tavern to home).*

Year 16 1997 *Towards The New American Religion. Summary #1: The first 19 years (1979-1998).*

Year 17 1998 *Two. The New American Religion.*

Year 18 1999 *Two. The New American Religion. A summary publication in the 19ᵗʰ year of the first 19 year cycle.*

Year 19 2000 *Two. The New American Religion. A summary publication in the nineteenth year of the first nineteen-year cycle.*

Introduction

Some Americans do not relate to any of the major foreign-based religious practices, such as Christianity,
Judaism, Islam, Hinduism, Buddhism, Confucianism or
Taoism. These spiritual and ethical systems emerged
from and reflect a cultural heritage that is often foreign
to many Americans. For example, certain Arab cultural
concepts, such as patriarchy, became incorporated into
Christianity, Judaism, and Islam; yet patriarchy seems to
conflict with the basic American belief that males and
females are equal co-creators of virtually everything we
see around us. Some of us long for an American religion
free of Arab and Eastern cultural concepts, a religion
that respects the cultural heritage and values that
Americans cherish: democracy, diversity, equality of
men and women, respect and tolerance for our neigh-
bors. We long for a religion free of the Old World
pagan concepts of gods, devils, priests, rabbis, sin,
redemption, heaven, and hell. What we want is a *truly*
American religion, as opposed to an American religion
such as Mormonism that is just another variation of an
Arab-based religion.

All valid religions report on the same spiritual
realms; there are not separate spiritual realms for the
Jews, the Christians, and the followers of Islam.

Unfortunately, the spiritual realms are so different from the human realms that we, as human beings, must try to describe the spiritual realms using metaphors or models commonly understood by the culture creating the religion. Since each culture is different, the metaphors describing the spiritual realms are also different, and thus the descriptions result in different religions. Any new American religion must be an accurate reporter of the spiritual realms, just like the foreign-based religions; only the metaphors will be different.

Why create a new religion? Doesn't the world have enough religions already? One reason to have a religion, any religion, is to have common, shared spiritual metaphors or models, which people can understand and refer to when talking about the spiritual realms. With shared metaphors it is possible to describe how to send and receive messages from the spiritual realms. Shared spiritual metaphors, derived from the culture, also allow children to be taught the values, morals, and ethics appropriate to the culture through the practice of the religion.

Many Americans will not choose this or any new religion, preferring instead to remain with the familiar Old World religions or with no religion at all. That is as it should be. No member of *Two* should try to change them. We clearly understand that it is from diversity that America gains much of her strength. Others, however, may be curious to see what a truly American religion might look like. For them and for us, what follows is a written summary of the first nineteen years of *Two: The New American Religion.*

Organization of This Summary Publication

The first three chapters of this book are rewritten, or what might more accurately be called remodeled, versions of ancient manuscripts. The word *remodeled* is meant to imply that the ancient manuscripts have been modernized, Americanized, and, in general, greatly changed. Words have been added and deleted, voicing changed, context and basic concepts modified, albeit lovingly as one might remodel and modernize the kitchen in a fine old home.

The ancient manuscripts that have been remodeled are as follows:

• The United States of America's *Declaration of Independence*, 1776 CE, for Chapter 1: A Declaration;

• An essay by a Roman named Plotinus, 205—270 CE, entitled *On The Good or The One*, for Chapter 2: Who We Are: The Basic Philosophy; and

• Poems by Jalal al-Din Muhammad Rumi, 1207—1273 CE, for Chapter 3: The Longing.

The Declaration of Independence has been used because it is an American tradition to publish this kind of a document when we Americans embark upon a major change from the Old World traditions. The Plotinus essay has been used because his philosophy had an influence on the early Christian religion and, thereby, allows for a comparison with Christianity. The Rumi poetry has been used because he is a revered Persian mystic of the Islamic religion and thus his writings allow for a comparison with Islam. These ancient manuscripts were also chosen because of the overall difficulty in writing about the spiritual realms. It is easier to select ancient writers who were good at writing about the spiritual realms and remodel their manuscripts rather than to start totally from the beginning. The original translations of the ancient manuscripts are in the three appendixes at the end of this book, for those who may be interested in comparing the original versions to the remodeled ones.

What is the symbolic meaning of the graphic image used throughout this book?

©

The *Two* Image*

The *Two* image is formed from two abstract symbols: the spiral and the star. The star symbol is meant to represent our Sun or, more abstractly, light. The spiral is meant to represent matter as it flows in a long, curved spiral path through our solar/matter system. The round form at the end of the spiral is meant to represent an accumulation of matter, such as a planet.

A Declaration

Chapter 1: "The Declaration" is a remodeled version of *The Declaration of Independence* from The United States of America, 1776 CE. See Appendix 1 for the text of the original version.

When
       in the course of human events
       it becomes necessary
       for a people
       to dissolve old religious bonds,
              which have for centuries
              helped them
              send and receive spiritual messages,
              and
              to create
                     among the religions of Earth
              a new religion
              designed specifically for Americans

       we feel obligated
       out of respect for our own history
       to document the causes.

We
hold this truth
to be self-evident:
    that
    all males and females
        are made by and from
        the Divine Sources
    and are thereby endowed,
        because of this creation process,
    with certain unalienable Rights.

Among those Rights are:
    The Right
    to send and receive spiritual messages
    directly
        to and from the Divine Sources
        for the purpose of determining
        personal behavior.
            (Realizing, of course, that
            personal behavior must also conform
            to the laws and traditions of
            the United States of America.)

In the past,
    to secure this Right
    people have
    created religions
        deriving the justification

to do so
from the knowledge that
the religions so created
    helped people
    learn techniques for
    sending and receiving spiritual messages.

But whenever any form of religion
exceeds this boundary
    it is the right of a people
        to alter
        or
        to abolish it
and
to create a new religion
    laying its foundation on such a principle
    and
    organizing its practices in such form
    as to them
    shall seem most likely
    to assist with
        learning techniques for
        sending and receiving spiritual messages.

Prudence, indeed,
will dictate that
    religions
        long established

should not be changed
for light and transient causes
and accordingly
>   all experience has shown
>   that the American people
>   are more disposed
>>   to tolerate their religious discontent,
>>   while it remains sufferable,
>>   than to
>>>   right themselves
>>>   by abolishing the forms
>>>   to which they are accustomed.

Nor have Americans been wanting
in attention
to our religious leaders
requests for money and devotion.

But when a long train
of Old World religious dogma
has caused a growing number of Americans
to live in unnecessary distress,
>   it is the right,
>   perhaps even the duty,
>   of a free people
>>   to throw off such religions
>>   and
>>   to provide

new guards against
future torment.

Such has been
        the patient suffering
        of many Americans
and
such is now
        the cause
        generating the initiative
        which compels the separation.

The history of the Old World religions
in the United States of America
is a history of
        repeated physical and emotional abuse to
        Americans
        and
        the forming of arbitrary rules
                all having in direct object
                the establishment of
                authority over an individual's personal
                behavior
                        extending far beyond
                        considerations of
                        spiritual communications.

To prove these allegations,
let the Facts be submitted
to an impartial world.

FACTS:
The Old World religions have tried to foster in
America the notion that:

- People are born with a special kind of sin,
- Homosexuality is unnatural,
- A person's knowledge about and use of
birth control should be restricted,
- Abortions sanctioned by American law are
immoral,
- Females have fewer rights than males.

There is hardly an American
that has not respectfully submitted,
      from time to time,
their concerns
to their religious leaders
      regarding the use of their authority
      to extend an unwarranted jurisdiction
      over their personal lives.

We have reminded the religious leaders
      of our shared circumstances
      of being here on Earth,

appealed to their sense of
native justice and magnanimity,
attempted to persuade
by the use of logic.

The religious leaders have been
practically deaf to these voices.
In every stage of these oppressions
Americans have petitioned for redress
in the most humble terms.

Their repeated petitions have been answered only by
repeated abuse
and
even more arbitrary rules.

A holy person
whose character is thus marked
by every act
which may define a Tyrant
is unfit to be a holy person
for a free people.

We must, therefore,
acquiesce in the necessity
of this separation
from the Old World religions
and

in creation of
a New American Religion.

We appeal to
the Old World religious leaders
for their understanding,
      having also created religions
      for their own cultures,
and
for the correctness of our intentions.

Therefore,

  in the names of the Divine Sources

  and

  with a firm reliance upon their protections

  and

  by the authority of a free people,

we do

solemnly publish and declare

that:

  any male or female from

  The United States of America,

   if they so desire,

  are hereby and from henceforth

   free

   to be totally dissolved of the Old World

   religions

   and

   are no longer bound by their covenants.

Who We Are, The Basic Philosophy

Chapter 2: "Who We Are: The Basic Philosophy" is a remodeled version of an ancient essay entitled "On the Good, Or the One" by a Roman named Plotinus, 205—270 CE. See Appendix 2 for the text of the original version.

11

CREATED THINGS TEND TO RESEMBLE THE SOURCES WHO CREATED THEM

Ordinary experience confirms that sons and daughters tend to resemble the father and the mother, the "sources" who created them. Because of the resemblance, it is possible to look carefully at a child and discover many obvious similarities between that child and his or her mother and father.

Other things, such as cars, tend to resemble the sources who created them in a less obvious manner. Nevertheless, by looking carefully at a car we can discover something about the sources that created it. For example, cars have two headlights. It would be correct to infer that the sources that created the car had two eyes. The size of the driver's seat, the distance to the pedals, the height from the seat to the roof, the adjustable range for moving the seat—all would imply the probable size range of the sources that created the car. And so on.

It is reasonable to assume that the Original Sources of males and females may not exactly resemble males and females in the same manner that cars do not exactly resemble the people who created the cars. Nevertheless, by looking carefully at males and females, something about the Original Sources may be inferred.

Two Basic Categories Of Living Things on Earth

There are two basic categories of living things on earth: males and females. These include male and female human beings, animals, birds, reptiles, amphibians, fish, and plants. While there are exceptions that are *neither* male nor female (such as simple one-celled organisms) and some that are *both* male and female (such as earthworms), these are the exceptions. Living things are more commonly either male or female.

THERE ARE TWO ORIGINAL SOURCES

If males and females are the two basic categories of living things on earth, and if created things tend to resemble their sources, then is reasonable to assume there are two Original Sources: one Original Source that is the source of the notion of male, and another Original Source that is the source of the notion of female.

Each Source Has Its Own Awareness

Each Original Source is thought to have a separate awareness which is the root of male consciousness and female consciousness. The one awareness appears to be similar to, but not exactly the same, as the other awareness. Each Original Source uses its awareness to jointly and intentionally create males and females and to give humans consciousness.

A thing is considered to have an awareness if it can:

(1) respond to a stimulus (for example, if a portion of the thing is damaged, the thing knows it);

(2) read and write a history (the DNA sequences that make up genes would be an example of a history); and

(3) manipulate its immediate environment (for example, form a protective coating, such as skin or bark, and change the environment inside to be different from the environment outside).

(For a more detailed discussion of awareness and consciousness see Chapter 4: Frequently Asked Questions, "What happens when a person dies?")

One Original Source or Two Original Sources?

Some will say, "I am a member of an Arab-based religion. My religion believes that there is only one Original Source of males and females, and He is called God. How does *Two* respond to that?"

There are at least four relevant responses to such a remark.

(1) The major Arab-based religions (such as Christianity, Judaism, and Islam) are patriarchal, reflecting the society in which they developed. One would not expect such a society to develop a religion in which a female was equally represented as a co-creator.

(2) If there were only one Original Source that contained both male and female in one entity, and if He created people in His own image, it would seem that this Original Source would create people that also contained both male and female in one individual: namely a hermaphrodite. Clearly, that is not the way people were created. A separate male and a separate female were created most likely to mimic the Original Sources.

(3) The idea of a "God" is a pagan concept that was commonly accepted by illiterate people two thousand years ago and readily adopted into the religions of the time. While most Americans accept the notion of spiritual entities, the concept of an all-powerful, all-knowing, all-seeing, all-creating "God" (in the Arab-based religion's sense of the word) is becoming widely questioned by a growing number of Americans.

(4) Even the "God" of the Arab-based religions does not claim to be made of nothing. God seems to be made of some kind of substances, frequently appearing as light or fire. It is the substances that were prior to God, what God is made from, that is of interest to *Two*. The *Two* religion seeks to understand the *Original* Sources, *the very first things that have a potential for an awareness.*

Additionally, if there was only one creator that contained both the source of male and the source of female, God could not be a *first* thing. Rather, God would be a *later* thing. God would be made of, at least, two separate, simpler, and earlier things; namely, the part of God from which originated maleness and the part of God from which originated femaleness. It would be possible to divide such an Original Source into the one part that contained the male essence and into a second part that contained the female essence, separating it into yet simpler components or parts.

Two is very different from the Arab-based religions in that it seeks to understand the simplest things that have the potential for an awareness.

THE SIMPLEST THINGS

While the two Original Sources may be thought of as the base roots of male and female, the Sources themselves could not actually be male or female. A male or a female is, again, a later thing, a complex thing made of simpler parts. The two Original Sources are the first things, the simplest of things having the potential for an awareness.

The Original Sources are simple but not plain; on the contrary, when combined they are rich with potential variety. After all, they are to be identified with all of the various and different kinds of males and females on earth. They are identified with the good *and* the bad in males and females. They are identified with awareness, the common awareness evident in all plants and animals. They are also to be identified with consciousness.

Consciousness, however, requires a brain and depends on an interaction between the one awareness associated with the one Original Source and the other awareness associated with the other Original Source. There can be no consciousness without a brain. The Original Sources do not have a brain and, therefore, do not possess consciousness. Judged only in relationship to the narrow confines of human consciousness, the Original Sources would appear to be "simple minded."

(For a more detailed discussion on this general subject see Chapter 4: Frequently Asked Questions, "What can be asked in a spiritual message?")

A MALE OR A FEMALE IS A COMBINATION

If a man and a woman want to create another human being, they combine parts of their bodies and create children from themselves. In the same manner, the two Original Sources also combine parts of themselves to create a male or a female.

A son or daughter is either male or female, and in this manner represents either the father or the mother. At the same time the son or the daughter is made from parts of both the mother and the father and thus contains both the mother and the father. The son or the daughter is thus fundamentally different from either the mother or the father.

In the same manner, a male or female is fundamentally different from either of the two Original Sources. A male or a female is made from both and thus contains *both* of the Original Sources.

This central fact is very confusing for humans. A human being is, at once, made *by* and *from* the two Original Sources, yet is unlike either Source since a human being contains both Sources.

THE TWO ORIGINAL SOURCES AS LIGHT AND MATTER

A human body, in its simplest description, is made of *complex heat* and *complex chemicals*. *Complex heat* can be described as combinations of individual radiation portrayed as various wavelengths in the electromagnetic spectrum, all of which may be loosely classified under the general category of *light*. *Complex chemicals* can be described as various combinations of the individual chemical elements that make up the Periodic Table of Elements, all of which may be loosely classified under the general category of matter.

Stated in these general terms, a human body is made of light and matter. Since the two Original Sources create males and females from themselves, it is possible to loosely describe the two Original Sources as light and matter.

COMMUNICATION WITH THE TWO ORIGINAL SOURCES

When we first try to create a mental image of the Original Sources as light and matter, we often find it difficult to grasp something so large, so seemingly unconfined, so utterly fantastic, so deceivingly common. Fearing that light and matter are nothing but dead substances, and in sheer dread of clinging to a lifeless idea, an image of the Original Sources as light and matter can easily slip away. Sometimes it seems easier to give up and be satisfied with the feeling of spiritual emptiness rather than to try to resolve this difficulty. This is why it is so important for people to understand how to send and receive spiritual messages.

The Human Mechanisms for Spiritual Messaging

Every person has two natural mechanisms for sending and receiving spiritual messages: (1) the quiet voice inside the head, and (2) the gut feelings in the pit of the stomach. People can *send* a spiritual message by forming words in their head (such as when a person is praying) or by forming gut feelings in the pit of their stomach (such as when a person is hoping for something). People can *receive* a spiritual message in the form of words that pop into their head and/or gut feelings that form in the pit of their stomach.

These two methods for sending and receiving messages to the spiritual worlds are the only connections that humans possess. Some human activity can confuse or scramble, and thereby diminish, the two forms of spiritual messaging. Such activities include taking mood-altering drugs, intense activity, hunger, tiredness, anger, sickness, and being in a negative state of mind. Most people have learned from common everyday experience that taking a mood-altering drug, such as alcohol, can create physical and mental confusion that easily scrambles any and all spiritual messages.

Some human activities, on the other hand, help to clarify and enhance spiritual messages. These activities include proper diet, meditative exercises, appropriate physical exercise, and paying attention to beautiful things.

Intentional Scrambling of Spiritual Messages

As strange as it may seem, as the clarity of the spiritual messages begins to improve it is common for a person to back away from them (especially when they start hearing the voice inside their head or the gut feelings in their stomach telling them not to do something). We, as Americans, are a very independent lot and do not want to be told what to do by anyone, or anything, even though it may be in our best interests. Consequently, people go through periods in their life when they want, consciously or not, to scramble almost all spiritual messages by any means available, usually by self dosing with mood-altering drugs. The mood-altering drugs commonly preferred by Americans, and those sanctioned by society at large, are nicotine, caffeine, alcohol, cocoa, cane sugar, and mood-altering prescription drugs (notably tranquilizers and antidepressants). These drugs at commonly used doses are sufficient to scramble most spiritual messages and keep one's communications "safely" and firmly only in the strictly human, earthly realms—where males and females are the uncontested masters of their own fate.

At the very same time, most Americans complain of feelings of spiritual emptiness. Eventually, with the advantage of age and hindsight, it is possible to put aside these self-isolating impulses. After doing so, one is then able, with dignity, to succumb to the curiosity to go exploring for the Original Sources.

How to Begin

People need to begin with what is already familiar: the quiet voice inside their head and what are usually called "gut," or "heartfelt," feelings. Begin by making subtle changes to your daily routine based upon whatever brings the best possible message clarity.

Most people can easily increase the spiritual message clarity by trying to bring their human body into the best possible balance. Balance here should be thought of as a balancing of all aspects of human life: body-chemistry balance, emotional balance, sexual balance, financial balance, and so on.

A balanced person will be sympathetically and consistently more "in tune," so to speak, with *both* of the natural frequencies associated with light and matter inside and all around them. Balancing the light and matter of one's body allows one to become an antenna to the signals from the Original Sources. Give your body the best possible chance to connect, to engage, and to resonate with the each of the Original Sources equally.

With these reasoned thoughts to act as a springboard, you may begin to nudge your body into an ever more balanced condition. Surround yourself with as much beauty as possible. Use meditation or other techniques to try to soften the boundaries of your body so as to be extended, open, and receptive. Seek a continuous daily encounter with *both of them*. Search for the clearest possible daily messages about anything and everything from the Original Sources. Pat yourself on the shoulder each time a clear message is received to compliment your body on a job well done.

Be prepared for the Original Sources to nag you into doing what is best for you but also trust that *they* will not punish you in any way if you do not listen. *They* understand the American need to have individual freedom, to have some room to experiment, even to do things that are bad for you. *They* understand these American needs so completely that *they* will even help you find some mischief to get into, if that is what you desire.

The Connection Between Body and Spiritual Messages

It is not altogether clear why Americans have taken such a long time to make the connection between the condition of their bodies and the clarity of spiritual messages. The clearest messages most Americans have ever had was when they were young children and went to bed on time, ate good meals at regular intervals, dressed properly to suit the weather, and exercised joyfully. Children generally have an open, wondering mind and body and have no problem thinking of the Original Sources as the voice of their teddy bear or doll or invisible companions. Later, as young adults, many Americans begin a descent into unhealthy living through peer pressure and laziness. Many begin the regular use of mood-altering drugs for what seems like good and important reasons: caffeine to stay awake, cocoa to be happy, sugarcane to have fun, alcohol to be sociable. Soon many of us become addicted to the drugs or the mood the drug created and require daily or weekly dosing. Thus begins the process of disconnecting. Through a significant part of adulthood, many Americans have scrambled spiritual messages because of their unbalanced life and unhealthy habits.

Even so, never do the Original Sources stop trying to send messages to us; never is a person really out of communication with the Original Sources. And yet somehow, while present, *they* seem remote to us. What you have turned away from, you cannot grasp.

Some Problems Created by the Arab-Based Religions

Looking back, perhaps the reason many Americans have not made the connection between the condition of their bodies and spiritual communication is that we have been influenced by the writings and teachings of the Arab-based religions, in particular Christianity. Christianity, either purposefully or circuitously, seems to encourage the idea that, when it comes to spiritual matters, the body is insignificant and the mind is very nearly everything. In fact, Christian saints who had their bodies mutilated, either by themselves or by others, were often depicted in spiritual ecstasy. Many have even come to assume that personal depravations such as fasting (eating only a few foods or none at all for certain periods of time) or ascetic living (such as wearing plain clothes or sleeping on a hard bed or living in isolation) actually improves one's spiritual life. Furthermore, if a person does something spiritually "bad," as defined by Christianity, some kind of penance is often required involving something physically punishing to the body (such as praying on your knees). Thus, many of us have come to feel that our body is, at best, irrelevant and, at worse, in conflict with a strong, spiritual life.

AN ALTERNATIVE PATH?

It may actually be possible to have a spiritually satisfying life through fasting or asceticism: "Complain enough and it will be given to you." However, it sounds a little like wanting to learn to make love standing up in a hammock; it may be possible, but why?

Such concepts not only seem misguided; they seem foreign to most Americans. An alternative path and probably the more user-friendly to Americans is to be a friend to your body. Give your body exactly what it needs to function properly. Treat your body with kindness, respect, and appreciation. Work with your body to achieve what is desired rather than to be at odds with it. This method will produce consistently clear spiritual messages day in and day out and is much more sympathetic to American life. Leave the depravation and asceticism to other cultures that have a cultural heritage for such behavior.

In addition, most Americans need some demystified, nonthreatening instructions. If the spiritual entities are presented as scary or frighteningly arbitrary and use punishments as tactics for obedience, you can be sure that most Americans will not want to go there. Most Americans just want some plain, simple instructions on how to send and receive spiritual messages clearly. Once the messages are clear, we can handle the rest.

WHO TO BLAME FOR AMERICA'S SPIRITUAL EMPTINESS

Somehow, it seems too easy to blame the Arab-based religions for Americans' feelings of spiritual emptiness. In the end, all the seeming impediments we must charge against ourselves. Let us use the sum total of all religious experiences as a learning tool, learning from both successes and mistakes. In the end, the goal is to find some spiritual methods specifically tailored to Americans: suited to American life, American values, American culture, and American temperament. Each person will, in the end, filter all the available information and find some personally acceptable method to connect to the spiritual realms.

WHAT DOES AN AMERICAN GET FROM CLEAR MESSAGING?

Clear messaging allows human life to become easier and less lonely.

Life becomes easier because the Original Sources will help set up the conditions to help you obtain the things you most desire. Good, clear spiritual messages are required to be at "the right place at the right time" to take maximum advantage of their assistance.

Young Americans commonly want to "do it by themselves" and so choose the more difficult path of trying to obtain everything they want by themselves. Unfortunately, the difficult path through the minefield of self-isolation is the only path possible for most young people. Be patient. Remember your own experiences. In addition, be patient with older Americans knowing that some Americans will die in old age without ever experiencing human life lived in concert with the spiritual realms.

Many, however, will make it through those difficult times. Besides, it is not an all or nothing thing. In the end, each American must decide how clear they want the communication to become and how much spiritual contact they want in their lives.

Clear messaging also help life become less lonely because the Original Sources of human life are here to contact and communicate with.

HOW DIFFICULT OR HOW LONELY DO YOU WANT YOUR LIFE?

Eventually, human beings figure out what they want. The better they treat their body, the clearer their daily spiritual messages become. The clearer the spiritual messages the easier and less lonely is a human life. Perhaps, at times, some do not want their life to be too easy or too pleasant. Maybe they think, "A little difficulty is more challenging, more interesting. Give me another piece of double-dark, chocolate cake with a large cup of espresso." Why not beat my body up a little bit and make life a little more interesting? Each person adjusts the way they treat their body and how alone they feel until they find just the right amount of challenge.

Some people, however, want to see precisely how *clear* the messages can ultimately become. For these spiritual athletes, life on earth with even slightly muddled spiritual messages will be a sinking, a defeat, a failing of their wings.

PEACE OF MIND

Sending and receiving messages to the One Source using the quiet voice is easier when your head is not filled with an excessive amount of self-generated words. Sending and receiving messages to the Other Source through gut feelings is easier when your gut feelings are not filled with an excessive amount of self-generated feelings and emotions. "Peace of mind," in *Two's* sense of the word, is not some far-off or difficult to attain enlightened state of being but rather an absence of excessive self-generated chatter and an ability to be a good receptor to the incoming spiritual messages. Having one's body balanced, well-rested, well-fed, in good physical condition, and without stress is the surest method to obtain peace of mind and is the method that lasts the longest. That does not mean that you should not experiment with other techniques to improve the messages.

Some may even endeavor to become reporters of the messaging techniques and of what was learned from the Original Sources in the messages. Such reporting is probably similar to that of the Old World philosophers, poets, prophets, and others, all known to be dramatically sending and receiving spiritual messages with at least one or the other or both of the Two Sources. From those messages they established the words used to report upon what they had learned. Others will choose to report nothing, instead, using their time to send and receive even more messages even more frequently. Perhaps they will be those who have learned much.

OTHER FACTORS AFFECTING THE CLARITY OF THE MESSAGES

The clarity of the mutual spiritual messages also depends, in some part, on two other factors: (1) an understanding of the spiritual realms; and (2) focus of attention.

Understanding of the Spiritual Realms. Clear spiritual messages depend in part on understanding the spiritual realms (how a person thinks of the Original Sources). When you think of the Original Sources as something other than yourself, the messages seems to go astray, like they are being sent to the wrong mailbox, because you are trying to communicate with an *other* thing. When you let go of the idea of "otherness," that the Original Sources are somehow different than you, then wherever you are, there *they* must be also. Thus, whenever you can put those ideas of "otherness" away, messages are not being sent off into space to some other unknown mailbox address, so to speak; you are messaging with *them* from the position that *they* are here with you. Knowing that *they* are you and all around you allows a person to address the messages properly, resulting in improved communication.

Focus of Attention. The clarity of spiritual messages also depends, in some part, on a person's focus of attention. Even though you are always with *them* and even though your body may be reasonably balanced, it is not possible to always communicate clearly with *them* if you are busy and focused upon other tasks. Right here, right now, occupied by writing or reading this we are withheld to some degree from being able to message with our spiritual Sources; gripped and fastened by this definite task, we are left with a diminished capacity for messaging.

The Things of Earth and "I" are Pleasant Also

Even though we are always together with the Original Sources, any number of things can separate us. To be cut off from *them* all the time is utter dissolution and loneliness for many. Nevertheless, even the most steadfast cannot always attend to the messages all the time, nor should a person even want to. The things of Earth are pleasant also. When a person is separate, it is possible to feel the unique exhilaration of a separate human life living on the surface of our beautiful planet Earth.

When a person is in contact again, the messages clear again, our time together with the Original Sources is attained; this is rest, rejuvenation, joy, and an end to separateness. Effectively together, with self-separation relaxed, there is an undeniable feeling of well being.

HOW TO NAME THEM

Strictly speaking, the Original Sources should not be called "they," "them," "light," "matter," "Original Sources," or any other name, so as not to preconceive what you will find. Hover, as it were, about these *entities*. Seek a statement of an experience of your own, something nearing your own human reality, realizing that at times you will be baffled by the enigma in which *both of them* dwell. *They* are both at once bizarrely unusual and commonly familiar. You will most assuredly recognize *them* when you encounter *them*. *They* are, after all, your celestial parents.

Since human words are insufficient to encompass the peculiarity of their realms and what *they* have initiated and accomplished, no name is apt. Nevertheless, it is in the American nature to want to give *them* some kind of a name. Thus, there is a certain rough fitness in naming them the "Two Sources."

Use this indication, then, as a kind of shorthand mark for the Original Sources with the understanding that it designates two unnamable entities each with the potential for awareness, from one of which came the idea of male and from the other of which came the idea of female.

THE AMERICAN PSYCHE

The American psyche seems to harbor a secret love for those ingenious Two Sources. This love is just waiting to bubble over at any moment and would apparently be thrilled to message frequently with *them*. Despite this, we Americans are rather easily lured by the courtship of the human sphere. We take up with another love, a mortal love of the pleasant American ways, leaving the celestial mother and father behind and becoming separate. Of course, no human being can actually be separate, although it can certainly seem like that at times.

As a young person, almost every American enjoys some of these exciting feelings of separateness. Gradually, however, the separateness begins to feel like loneliness. As we grow older, it is common to begin a search to find the companionship of one's celestial roots and the associated peace, striving to blend the mortal life smoothly now with the spiritual life. All of this may sound superfluous to young people. However, there will usually come a time in older age when it is understood to be that of winning what is most desired. When in that state of mind, a human being typically basks in the wonder of life when messaging with the Two Sources;

thus restored, feeling the pure essences of life, a person is soothed and calmed.

Sending messages back and forth to the spiritual realms seems to be a native human activity; through these messages life is made easier and less lonely, beauty brought forth along with fairness and moral quality. For all these things, human beings are pregnant when they have been filled from contact with the Two Sources. Life in contact with the Two Sources allows people to communicate with their first and final states. From *them* we come and to *them* we will return; in between those two events, it is possible to comprehend the enormity of how males and females came to be.

What is the Nature of the Spiritual Messaging?

Strictly speaking, when receiving a message, a person does not actually hear a sound. Nor does the stomach actually feel a feeling. It is closer to sensing or intuition led by the common experiences of hearing and feeling. The messages are something subtle, gentle, undramatic, a contact with an order always known, a reacquaintance, something discovered that every American has already known for a very long time.

When receiving a message, the person comes to know himself or herself as being a part of Two Sources—the male and female part of a person connected with those same celestial parts. It is as though you are having an encounter with the sources of your very natures. It is a knowing of one's self restored to its pure roots, an instantaneous knowing of who we are. It is very nearly impossible to write about the experience and not talk in duality as though there is a "speaker" and a "hearer," a "toucher" and a "touched". However, there should be no speaking of hearing and feeling rather, a writer should boldly state, "It is the achievement of similar things together."

In this communication, there is no beholding of an object nor any tracing of a distinct form; *a person is not separate* from the source of the message. The person feels changed somehow, no longer in a separate bodily realm; it is the feeling of being merged with something larger.

It is easy to imagine that any human being, balanced or unbalanced, who sends or receives a message, no matter how clear or scrambled, has achieved a contact with *them*, sunken into *them*, together with *them*. For on these planes, things that communicate *are* in contact. Only by refusing to communicate or intentionally scrambling the communication can the link be broken.

A Story That Cannot Actually Be Told

The story of the spiritual messages, in some sense, baffles telling: a person must focus attention elsewhere and disconnect from the messaging in order to do the very act of reading or writing a book. Thus, the impression that people are separate creeps into the story, and the narrative has fallen short of the essential understanding, which is to know *them* and us as the same things.

SIGNS

It would seem that, having made contact with *their* inner sanctuaries, a person's first thought would be to leave the human realms behind as though they were unimportant in the great scheme of things. On the contrary, the human realms become even more precious when disconnected from *them*, knowing that *they* have created this amazingly impressive array of things on Earth. Realizing that, the next impulse is to take a closer look at it all to see how *they* did it and to see how it might be refined!

Things here on earth are signs of *their* work. Beauty is *their* signature: an authentic fingerprint of *their* involvement. One has only to search for beauty to find the threads of *their* story. Perhaps someone reading only the signs of beauty may more easily connect and make clear the messages. Certainly, instructions such as in this book or in any other book are not necessary. Those uninstructed and unaccompanied are able to participate in the messaging. They will learn their own methods, since "like will have contact with like," and so they learn the messaging system without words or instructions.

For others, it is important that the instructions be written down somewhere and available to be read from time to time, for people who enjoy writing and reading books, what can I say!

THE PURPOSE OF AN AMERICAN LIFE

If sending messages back and forth is so delightful, why not spend the rest of your life messaging? The answer is simple: Americans are drawn back by what seems to be the very purpose of an American life—*to refine the creation.* Most Americans greatly admire and respect the things the Two Sources have created. However, the work does not seem finished: it appears to us to need some refinement. *Americans are just arrogant enough to actually think we can make the original creation better.* After all, there are still living things suffering. Americans are perfectly suited to this task: we are creative, hard working, and we love to test our own refinements. Sometimes the refinements we make to the creation are perfectly done. At other time, the refinements are entirely wrong. Most things fall somewhere in the middle. We learn; we constantly learn from the process of refining and testing.

Sometimes the work of refinement and testing pulls us out of balance; the work then begins to feel like a burden and we lose our clear messages and begin to flounder around unproductively. When this happens, we need to know the way to re-create the balance and to re-establish the clear messages again and refocus our work. This done, we are once more lightened of the seeming burden, and we can get back to the work of refining the creation with pleasure.

To some people, clear communication with the Two Sources and a lifetime spent refining the creation can be seen as the life of a content, productive, and blessed human being—a life in pleasant communion with the things of Earth and with the Two Sources.

The Longing

Chapter 3: "The Longing" is a collection of remodeled versions of some ancient poetry by Jalal al-Din Muhammad Rumi, 1207—1273 CE. See Appendix 3 for the original versions.

How is it with our human eyes
at first
    as young people
we see
    only the outer shell of our world
    and
    ourselves as separate from
    our Sources?

Eventually as older adults
we begin to marvel
at the male and female parts
of our own body
    and from there
begin the journey
to find
our roots.

For years, trying numerous variations
of the Arab-based religions,
    we tried to send messages
    to the spiritual realms.

Caught up with
the Old World religious images
    it was difficult to maintain a
    consistent contact with *Them.*

We could not decide
what to do.

Unable to find a way,
we began to listen to
    our quiet voice
        and
    our heartfelt feelings.

Then we walked outside,
    out beyond ideas
    of gods and goddesses,
to a field.

There we met
our Two Sources.

We've heard it said
a saint, a pope, a priest,
a minister, a rabbi or a preacher
    can open a window
        from the human realm
        to
        the spiritual realm.

But,
if there is no wall,
    there is no need
    for fitting such a window
        (or a latch).

All day long we think about it,
then at night we say it,
    "Who are we?
    Where did we come from?
    What are we supposed to be doing?"

We Americans are like a bird sitting
in this beautiful aviary
with wings able to fly,
but
    sitting still, asking,
    "Who is it now speaking these words into the air?
    Who hears this voice?
    Who wrote these words on this page?
    Who looks out with these eyes?"

We cannot stop asking
and
we enjoy the search
for the answers;
    it has become our life,

Last night, again we asked this one question,
"Who are we?"

> *We are the dust you stirred up*
>   *asking that question.*
> *We are the lips, the air*
>   *and the pale yellow light*
> *you used just now*
> *to read and speak these words.*

Sometimes, these answers
seem like no answers at all;
    we want less puzzling answers.

If we could understand,
    we would say the answers simply
    without confusion.

A young bird's wings beat air,
wanting to fly, becomes tired,
    sleeps and waits to practice another day.

A campfire gives in to rain.
But we cannot stop exploring.

When we are asleep,
    it feels like we lose our contacts
    with the both of you
    and we want to hold you back.

We worry
    we won't have someone to talk to
    and breathe with.

Don't you understand
    you are some kind of food for us.
You are the reason for our work.

When we sleep,
    the bottle is corked,
    and
    sitting on the table.

If someone should happen upon us
and see us without the both of you
    they would pity us
    as though we were a lost child
    and pat us gently on the head.

It has been said that the moment Americans
began writing love songs
    we began searching for
    the sources of those songs,
        not knowing how blind that was.

Lovers don't finally meet somewhere,
They are with each other all along.

During the day it seemed as though
we were playing music
with the both of you.

At night
    we seemed to be sleeping
    in the same bed.

We weren't really conscious day or night.

We were thinking
    we were with our Sources.

But now we know:
    we are our Sources.

We are rainwater
    down into the ground.

We are a daisy
    up into the air.

We are
    a salad,
    a fish,
    a tree covered with leaves,
    a dog fetching a stick.

Knowledge
    of the Two Sources
seemed to be hidden
within these things

until one day it is as though
we have cracked them open
    and can
        at last
see who we are.

Lo, we are always together
with the Two Sources.

When we look for *them*,
    we need only look into our eyes,
      look into the thought and the feeling of looking,
    look nearer to ourselves than ourselves.

There is no need to go outside of
    what we are.

Since we each have come to know
who we are,
    a game goes on.
We move
    and the Two Sources respond.
They move
    and we respond.
It is almost like a game.

But pause from the game for a moment;
    see how we are bringing furniture to this place
    and setting up house-keeping
        so we can all live comfortably
        here together.

We have come to know
and to feel that
the both of you are in love:
    cows grazing contentedly
        on a sacred table of grass,
    ants whispering in the moist belly of earth,
    mountains mumbling an echo.

If the both of you were not in love,
    there would be no brightness,
    the side of hills no grass upon it,
    and
    the oceans everywhere would come to rest.

Sometimes, we Americans worry about losing our
bodies when we die.
        Eventually though, we learn not to worry
        because
                anything we lose comes around again
                in another form.

The child weaned from mother's milk
now eats
        blueberries,
        orange cantaloupe
        and yellow peaches.

Besides,
        every day when we breathe
        part of our body is lost
                floating away on each breath.

The plants take this in
        and we take in
                what the plants have lost
                in their breathing.

We might say
        last night part of me was
                a maple tree,
                a bed of flowers,
                a field of green grass.

Frequently Asked Questions

Contents for Frequently Asked Questions

MEMBERSHIP

HOW CAN I BECOME A MEMBER OF TWO: THE NEW AMERICAN RELIGION?

Members of the *Two* religion share a common belief and/or feeling that there are two fundamental Sources active in our solar/matter system. One Source is responsible for the notion of male, and the Other Source is responsible for the notion of female. It does not matter what these Two Sources are called: light/matter, yin/yang, him/her, they/them, republican/democrat, socialist/capitalist. And because there are two Sources, there can never be one truth. There will always be at least two truths, two different points of view. One truth represents the preferred reality of the One Source, and a second truth represents the preferred reality of the Other Source.

The Two Image

If you are comfortable with the common belief, then to become a member simply wear the *Two* image somewhere on your body. If you wear the *Two* image in plain sight, perhaps as a pendant, pin, or emblem on a T-shirt or hat, it indicates that you would enjoy talking to others about *Two*. See copyright information in the Introduction of this book or at the Web site: *www.NewAmericanReligion.org* If you wear the *Two* image hidden, it indicates that you prefer to remain secretive about your membership. For example, you could print and sign the following *Two* membership card, and carry it in your wallet or purse.

Two: The New American Religion

©

Name _____

Member since

Two members should be able to settle out into two broadly defined groups: (1) research members, and (2) practicing members. Each type of member would serve very important but different functions.

Research Members.

The research members use no particular guide to determine their lifestyle. These are the people who are unaccustomed or unwilling to learn by "reading the instruction manual." These are the kind of people that generally jump right in and like to learn through trial and error and experimentation. Research members experiment with various lifestyles and various drugs, using their own bodies and their own lives as research subjects. They try to send and receive spiritual messages the best that they can. Furthermore, it is hoped that they will try to document their lives either in a local context, through discussions with family and friends, or in a larger context, such as the arts, so that others may see and learn from their lifestyles. Some research members will serve as examples of how to make your life very difficult and/or very lonely. Each generation must learn the consequences of certain behaviors, not from being told by the older generations, but by seeing the results first hand from their peers.

Practicing Members.

The practicing members use the latest techniques available from *Two* to determine their lifestyle. These are the people who are inclined to read user manuals. The practicing members also use their own bodies and their lives as test examples. The practicing members represent the state of the art in personal spiritual messaging. It is hoped that they share what they have learned with other members.

Both kinds of members are very important. There should be no attempt to make either kind of member feel as though they should be the other kind of member.

DEATH

WHAT HAPPENS WHEN A PERSON DIES?

In the past, when a child asked an adult, "Where do babies came from?" it was not uncommon for the adult to respond by saying, "Babies come from the stork." This simplistic and somewhat romantic answer did have one advantage: it was easy to understand. Today most children are taught the actual answer of where babies come from, including the much more complicated details and accompanying discussions of hormones, menstrual cycles, sperm, ovulation, and venereal diseases. The actual story turns out to be more miraculous and more fantastic than if the stork story had been literally true. The actual story, because of the disease possibilities, is *also* a little scary.

Similarly, for most of the last two thousand years, when an adult has asked, "What happens to me when I die?" it has not been uncommon for a holy person to say, "You go to heaven or hell, depending." This also is a simplistic and romantic answer that is easy to understand. The actual answer, in the same manner as the baby/stork story, is more complicated, considerably more miraculous, more fantastic, and *also* a little scary. Here is why.

Some Background.

Imagine that in our solar/matter system, under certain common conditions, matter naturally bursts into light (think of a burning log in a fireplace). Under certain common conditions, light naturally condenses into matter (think of sunlight falling on the leaf of a tree and being converted into sugar). When matter bursts into light an awareness arises. When light condenses into matter another awareness arises. The one awareness is similar to but not exactly the same as the other awareness. An awareness cannot be separated from the conversion process or from the physical presence of light or matter. From a human point of view, and expressed in the context of light and matter, a "living thing" is generally a thing that can convert both light into matter and matter into light in a continuous and interactive process, all within one entity.

Light and matter each use their awareness to create males and females. Light and matter also create consciousness. Consciousness is a complicated interplay between the awareness associated with light and the awareness associated with matter inside a brain. It is not possible to have consciousness without a brain.

Awareness versus Consciousness.

If a person is having difficulty distinguishing between awareness and consciousness, think of a tree. When light and matter are a tree, they have the awareness associated with light and the awareness associated with matter but no brain and, therefore, no consciousness. Yet, a tree can easily be aware of wet and dry, light and shade. A tree can even be aware of insects. Further, a tree can make decisions based upon this information (e.g., whether to grow more roots in a certain area of the soil, what kind of leaves to grow based on the available sunlight, and what kind of chemicals to secrete based on insects). Light and matter are similar to a tree in that they have awareness but no consciousness. Being human, we tend to think of consciousness as being the "really big deal," but awareness is actually the bigger deal in our solar/matter system.

Light and matter, each using their awareness, created our solar/matter system after some trial and error. Our solar/matter system converts matter into light, near the center, at the sun. The light, as it moves outward, condenses back into matter. Much of the condensed matter that does not wind up in planets or moons eventually follows a long spiral path into the black hole that feeds the sun, to be converted back into light, thus forming a large recycling system. Our solar/matter system, accordingly, is a huge system capable of converting light into matter and matter into light in one continuous interactive process, thus continuously producing the awareness associated with matter and the awareness associated with light in one large entity. Our solar/matter system, therefore, conforms to the above definition of a "living thing."

Furthermore, there is no important difference, other than size, between a living thing, such as a tree, and our solar/matter system. The only significant difference between a living thing with a brain, such as a person, and our solar/matter system is that people have the consciousness produced by a brain.

The solar/matter system that light and matter created is thus everywhere alive with awareness, although that is not the most accurate way to state it. To call our solar/matter system "alive" is to leave the impression that life is somehow added to it. A more accurate image is that our solar/matter system is created in such a way that the awareness associated with matter and the awareness associated with light are constant, fundamental features.

Consider Trees.

A tree, while it is alive, has within itself the one awareness associated with the tree converting light into matter and also the other awareness associated with converting matter into light. As long as these conversions function in a balanced or sustainable manner, the tree may be said to be alive.

Consider now an insect, perhaps an ant, living inside the tree. The ant has the one awareness associated with converting light into matter and also the other awareness

associated with converting matter into light. As long as
these conversions function in a balanced or sustainable
manner, the ant is alive and the ant will feel like it pos-
sesses its own personal awareness. However, when the
ant dies some part of the light and matter of the ant is
very quickly absorbed by the next larger environment
(which is the tree). As the body of the ant rots, the tree
gradually absorbs the remaining light and matter of the
ant. Because of the absorption processes, some of the
particular experiences of the ant can be "remembered" by
the tree. The ant, at the moment of death, will lose its
personal awareness and an instant later will be part of the
tree's personal awareness. The transition from experiencing personal awareness as the ant to experiencing personal awareness as the tree is smooth and instantaneous.

When the tree dies, the awareness associated with
light and the awareness associated with matter formed
by the tree when the tree converted light into matter
and matter into light ceases to exist in an interactive
way. The tree ceases to have its personal awareness as
a separate entity and becomes part of the adjoining
environment's awareness. As the body of the dead tree
rots and falls down, producing heat (light) and organic
material (matter), these may be used to produce grass
and flowers. The light and the matter from the tree
used to make the grass and flowers will also contain a
little bit of the memory of the experience of being that

particular tree and that particular ant. All things thus will eventually have some knowledge of all other things.

Now Consider People.

When a person dies, the awareness associated with light and the awareness associated with matter that was formed when the person converted light into matter and matter into light ceases to exist in an interactive manner. The consciousness produced by the person's brain and the personal feeling of awareness also, for the most part, cease to exist. All people will "die" in this manner. Eventually, the person's heat and body, like the tree and the ant, will be recycled back into light and matter elsewhere in our solar/matter system. The recycled light and the recycled matter from the person will carry a little bit of the memory of having been the particular person that they were. The change from the experiences of awareness as a person to the experiences of awareness as something else in our solar/matter system will be continuous and uninterrupted (somewhat like changing channels on the TV). To the person, it will not seem as though he or she has died, only changed form somehow.

Here is the startling and, when you think about it in a certain manner, the somewhat scary part: As long as our solar/matter system remains what it is, it is not possible to die a final and absolute death without becoming a part of some awareness somewhere.

It is appropriate to recognize and celebrate this enormous achievement over an absolute death by the Two Sources (See Preferred Practice #4, Vernal Equinox celebration).

What are the choices after your human death?

Nearly all religions and primitive societies recognize a period after a person dies when some rudimentary parts of your human personality can be confined and held intact while completely detached from your former body. For most people the period is generally brief, frequently considered to be less than a few days, with some exceptions. Let us call this period of time the "after death transition period". During the after death transition period, it would appear that you have four basic choices:

- Move toward the light and to disbursement;
- Move toward the matter and become part of some other living thing on earth;
- Hang around somewhere in between the light and the matter; or
- Do not attempt to confine what is left of you.

During the after death transition period, you (the word "you" is used in this section in an other-than-normal context) probably will be only a gossamer, wispy collection of light and matter barely held together. You will most likely have only awareness and no consciousness, since you have no brain. You will probably be able to be aware of things like light, darkness, and movement. You

will probably be able to make choices based upon awareness, but the choices, by human standards, will probably
seem to be primitive, yes/no kind of choices. You will
probably be able to move around by navigating wind current and magnetic fields.

Moving toward the light.

You will undoubtedly first notice the light. The light,
which is our sun, is a powerful swirling furnace near the
center of our solar/matter system that has a tendency to
draw loose matter toward it. If you stay confined and do
nothing else, you will probably be drawn toward the sun.
Once you hit the sun and swirl around for some time,
you will probably be exploded out in all directions. The
former parts of you will be disbursed throughout our
solar/matter system. If you always wanted to go to Mars
or Venus, this is definitely the path for you. If you consider life on earth to be a "vale of tears" or "an unending
cycle of painful rebirth", this is definitely the path for
you. If you are an explorer and want to "see what is out
there", this is definitely the path for you.

The light will seem to have awareness. The awareness
of the light will seem to be similar to your father, hus-
band, or some other strong male figure in your life. If
the remembrance of a male figure is a pleasant experience for you, you may be "emotionally" drawn toward
the light.

Moving toward the matter.

Immediately after your human death, the big clump of matter, which will be earth, will be in the opposite direction of the light. You should be able to identify it by the awareness of a slightly cooler body nearby. It will probably be a little more difficult to hang around earth since the tendency will be to float slowly toward the light. If your intention is to experience life on earth again, you will want to move away from the light toward the darkness. Yes, the darkness. There is nothing to fear in the darkness, it is the same kind of dark matter from which you are currently made. If, for example, you want to try to live as a tree, position your gossamer essence as near as possible around a tree. As you get near to the tree and if the tree is not dormant, you will be aware of a sucking feeling which is the tree absorbing light and matter into itself. The sucking will absorb some of what is left of you and some part of you will be a tree. If you want to be a bird, try to die in the spring when the birds are laying eggs. During the after death transition period, try to move your gossamer essence towards a bird's nest. You should be aware of a significant sucking near the baby birds or the eggs. Move to allow your essence to surround the young hatchlings or the eggs. The sucking will absorb some of what is left of you and some part of you will be a bird. If you want to try human life again, in the same manner, move toward a baby or pregnant woman and allow your essence to be absorbed. Absorption can, of course, happen with any size of living thing. However, the smaller the living thing the greater the influence of the gossamer essence.

The matter will also seem to have awareness. The awareness of the matter will seem to be similar to your mother, wife, or some other strong female figure in your life. If the remembrance of a female figure is a pleasant experience for you, you may be "emotionally" drawn toward the matter.

If your intention is to return as much of you as possible to another human life experience and you want to try to be aware of what has happened, *Two* is trying to develop a mechanism for you to leave a message to yourself that can be read in your new life. If enough of you has been absorbed into the new human life, you should be able to recognize the message you left for yourself. *Two* calls these messages "Remembrance Messages"; see the Web site *www.NewAmericanReligion.org Remembrance Messages* button for more information.

Hang around somewhere in between.

If you cannot decide or if you are frightened by the first two choices, make it your intention to stay away from the light and the matter until you are ready to decide. Some religions seem to suggest that you may be able to remain in this in-between condition for quite some time. You probably will have to be careful not to get to close to living things on earth because you could be sucked in and absorbed by them (try hanging out in an old abandoned house somewhere), or too close to the light because you could be sucked into the sun and disbursed. It will probably seem as though you are in a kind of limbo. It, too, could be a very interesting experience.

IMPROVING THE CLARITY OF SPIRITUAL MESSAGES

WHAT IS TO BE GAINED BY BRINGING MY BODY INTO BALANCE?

It is reasonable to ask, "What will I gain by trying to bring my body into balance by giving up mood-altering drugs and following a nutritious eating plan?" The answer is "nothing new", only better functioning of what you already have. You have always had the quiet voice inside your head, as everybody does. You have always had the gut feelings, as everybody does. However, the more balanced your body, the easier it is for you to:

(1) Receive spiritual messages,

(2) Act upon the spiritual messages, and

(3) Send spiritual messages.

Receiving spiritual messages.

It is more difficult to understand spiritual messages from *them* when your body is unbalanced due to mood-altering drugs, poor diet, or by being tired, anxious, scared, depressed, or lonely. Such conditions cause the words to seem garbled and unclear and the gut feelings to seem vague and indistinct. The understanding is made more difficult if the word or feeling occurs in the middle of a huge number of self-generated words and feelings. In addition, you will have more difficulty quieting an unbalanced mind and body.

Acting upon the spiritual messages.

It is not enough to only receive the message. You must receive it, understand it, and be willing to act upon it, trusting that it is in your own best interest to do so. For example, suppose you are leaving the house in the morning and have forgotten to take your lunch. Suddenly, some words pop into your head such as "You have forgotten your lunch," or you have the "forgotten my lunch," feeling in the pit of the stomach. First, you have to be able to understand these words or feelings. If all you have is a vague notion that you have "forgotten something," chances are you will walk out of the house and forget your lunch. Let us suppose that you understand the words or feelings. You have to understand well enough to *actually* go back in the house and pick up your lunch. In this example, you would be foolish not to. But what if it is late at night and your body is sending you messages, both in words and feelings, that it wants to go to bed and you ignore the received messages. The communication may be clear, in the second example, but you are not always able or willing to act upon the messages even though life experience has taught you repeatedly that you usually pay a price for ignoring the messages. Sometimes people refuse to act upon the messages out of defiance or immaturity. Learning to act upon spiritual messages is, to a large degree, a process facilitated by life experiences. Most people will say that they seldom learn from the first bad experience. The older you become, the easier it is to listen and act on the messages, because you have had more experience with the consequences of not doing so.

Sending spiritual messages.

Spiritual messages become a dialogue, instead of just a monologue, when you can originate messages. This opens up a person's ability to communicate with the Two Sources directly and also with other males and females at an entirely different level. If you can only receive the messages, the communication is like a one-way street. When you can talk back or ask questions, it is more like a dialogue and considerably more interesting than just listening. It is the difference between listening to the radio and talking on the telephone. A problem with sending the messages is learning how to differentiate from a serious message, from which you expect a response, and a casual thought or feeling which, as far as you are concerned, requires no action from *them*. Some religious communities develop a special body posture, such as kneeing and holding the palms of the hands together, when a serious message is being sent. Finding a place to kneel is problematic. Here is a much easier and well-established special body posture for important contact with the Two Sources. Touch your stomach with one open hand and the top of your head with the other open hand when you want to send a very serious message. A preferred and more advanced method is to develop quietness inside your body so that messages to be sent are clearly differentiated from internal messages not intended to be sent.

Everyone seems to have all three parts of the communication naturally by the age of two or three. It is amusing to witness children first start to hear the quiet voice inside their head. They are often confused as to where the voice is coming from, and frequently attribute the voice to an invisible playmate or to a stuffed doll or toy. The only thing that really changes from that early childhood experience as we grow older is our ability to control, by balancing our body, the clarity of the messages received, acted upon, and sent.

What can be asked in a spiritual message?

What kinds of questions can be asked in a spiritual message? Is it possible, for example, to send the following spiritual message, "What is the square root of ten?" And if so, what kind of an answer will you expect to receive? Yes, it is certainly possible to send that kind of a message. However, before it is possible to describe what kind of an answer you will likely receive, it is necessary to understand some background information.

Humans can do some things (such as mathematics) better than the Two Sources. Always remember, the Two Sources are not all-powerful, all-knowing Gods. As far as anyone can tell, the Two Sources cannot calculate the square root of ten and will not be able to send you a communiqué with the answer. That does not mean they will not try to answer your question. Typically, they will try to set up a situation in which you can find the answer yourself. This can take several different forms.

A favorite of the Two Sources seems to be to put a person in contact with someone who can answer the question. Often the person who can answer the question seems to almost "bump" into you as if by chance. These "chance" encounters, of which almost everybody is familiar, are one of the pleasant facets of human

existence. The Two Sources are very skilled at bringing
two people in need together at just the right time.
When you ask a technical question, you need to be
prepared to be brought into contact with someone who
can answer the question. This technique is possible
only with another person who is also willing to follow
their inner voice and/or gut feelings. If either are
unwilling, the contact never happens. It really takes
two people who can both act upon, either consciously
or unconsciously, spiritual messages.

Another method is to put you in contact with a book,
a periodical, a television program, or a lecture that can
provide the answer. This process is subtle. For example,
while at a friend's house, you might be urged for what
may seem like a strange reason to look at a magazine on
their coffee table. Or perhaps, a friend will ask if you are
going to attend a certain lecture. It is easy to miss these
contacts if you are not open to them. When your body
is unbalanced, paying attention to what is going on
around you requires a considerable conscious effort. You
have to pay attention by constantly reminding yourself
to pay attention. If you stop reminding yourself, you
may not pay attention. A major benefit of balancing
your body is that you pay attention in a more natural
way without having to remind yourself. Paying attention
is a part of the neutral state of a balanced body, the state
you can be in most of the time.

One might ask, "How can the Light and Matter, who created everything, not know everything?" Here is the answer, illustrated in a make-believe conversation.

Your home computer asks you the following question, "Who created me?"

You reply, "Human beings."

Your computer says, "You are a human being; how many calculations can you do in a second?"

You reply, "Perhaps I can do one calculation every ten seconds or so depending on how difficult the calculation."

"But I can do tens of thousands, sometimes even millions of calculations every second," says your computer. "Surely whomever created me can do at least that many calculations and probably a lot more. I do not believe humans created me, I think I must have been created by some super something or other."

It is not unusual for humans to expect that whatever created them must be better in *every* way, maybe even omnipotent. Yet, this is not true. There are some things that humans can do better than the Two Sources who created them, not unlike the computer example. It was remarkable that the Two Sources created something that is, in some ways, better than *they* are. This is not unlike human beings creating computers.

There are many questions, especially technical questions, that the Two Sources will not be able to directly answer. There are also many questions, on the other hand, that *they* will be able to answer but for which there are inadequate metaphors. For example, let us reuse the computer example in a little different context. Pretend that you ask your home computer, "How do you work?" You might imagine that the computer would begin by explaining how it works by discussing 1s and 0s and machine-level programming languages. The 1s and 0s, however, are metaphors so that humans can understand what is really going on, which is tiny pieces of material are being set to a positive or negative charge. The computer only knows what it is doing, which is setting or unsetting charges and then moving streams of electrons down ever-changing pathways. Now imagine that you have never heard about the metaphor of the 1s and 0s, and you know nothing about programming languages. You ask the computer to explain how it works, and the computer is trying to explain about setting positive and negative charges and changing pathways. The computer "knows" perfectly well what is going on, or so we are assuming in this example, but may not be able to tell you in a way that you can understand.

Check it out. Send a spiritual message to the Two Sources asking to know how your digestive system works. This is a good example of something that Light and Matter can do easily. *They* know exactly how it works, but *they* will have an enormously difficult time explaining it you. Here is another example, ask the Two Sources, "How did *both of you* come to create males and females?" The Two Sources worked together to do it, *they* know how *they* did it, but *they* will have difficulty explaining it to a human being in a manner that can be understood. In fact, the only way the Two Sources can explain it to a person is to try to use shared metaphors for which both *they* and humans have worked out a common understanding. If you only understand simple metaphors (for example "God did it"), that will be the best *they* can do. If you understand something about evolution, then the Two Sources will be able to use that metaphor and explain in a little more detail. You can understand more and more details as the shared metaphors between you and the Two Sources grow in complexity.

Dream Queries.

There is yet another method by which the Two Sources can answer a request: through *dream queries.* Here is how it seems to work. If you ask a question that the Two Sources do not know the answer to or if the Two Sources are having a difficult time finding a metaphor that you can understand, *they* will ask the question of someone who might know the answer in a dream while the person is sleeping. The person responds in the dream, and the answer is transmitted to you— usually as a gut feeling or by words popping into your head, often when you first awake or early in the morning when you are relaxed, perhaps taking a shower. Conversely, you may also be used as a source of answers for other people's questions. You can tell the difference between ordinary dreaming and these dream queries. During a dream query, you are asked a specific question. Moreover, as strange as this may sound, you are unable to lie or even exaggerate while you are responding. You will seem to be able to only tell the truth and give only as much information as you are sure is correct. The routine is very formal. You will be asked the question, you respond, and the dream query is over. If your head is fairly clear, you will know when it is happening and what is going on. When people are first conscious of these dream queries, they are often surprised by them, by the formality and the abruptness. Later a person will become quite comfortable with them and even enjoy being of help. It seems like a very good system.

Occasionally the format of the dream query will be used by the Two Sources to find out what you truly want. It usually concerns a subject for which you have been inconsistent or at cross purposes in your spiritual messages. The Two Sources use the dream query to ask what you really want. Under these circumstances, you will reveal your true desire. When the question is asked, you may be curious yourself as to what the answer will be and may even enjoy hearing the answer since you are not sure what you will say! Be forewarned, however, that you might be surprised by your answer.

WHAT IS THE "NEUTRAL" FEELING?

As the human body approaches a chemical balance, the feeling associated with that state could be referred to as the *neutral feeling.* The neutral feeling is similar to feelings one might associate with a content or pleasant feeling. It is a feeling that comes about automatically without effort. In this condition, a person experiences no particular emotions whatsoever. While the condition may be accurately described as emotionally "neutral," it does imply that a person does not have access to their full range of emotions. Some people have asked if you feel "good" when your body is in chemical balance. The answer is *no*, you do not feel good. Chocolate makes you feel good. Coffee and cigarettes make you feel good. As your body approaches a chemical balance and you experience the neutral feeling, you just feel *ordinary*—neither good nor bad, neither high nor low, just ordinary. This does not mean that your emotions have disappeared; rather the emotions seem to be at rest. A person can listen to some upbeat rock and roll music and, in a few moments, feel high. On the other hand, a person can listen to a "Requiem Mass for the Dead" and feel low. However, the minute you turn off the music, and if you give no more energy to staying high or low, your emotions begin to return naturally to the neutral feeling. When the human body is out of chemical balance, a person must give energy to become "centered" or balanced. When you stop devoting energy to staying balanced, you gradually return to being high or low, the place from which you started. When the body is chemically balanced, you must give energy to be high or low. When you stop devoting energy to being high or low, you gradually return to this neutral state.

ARE THERE METHODS, OTHER THAN EATING PROPERLY, FOR BALANCING THE BODY?

Yes, it is possible for a person to get into a kind of balance, even when the chemistry of the body may be unbalanced, through the use of a personal chant (such as a mantra) or group chant (such as a religious service). Here is basically how to do a personal chant. Get into a comfortable position, sitting or lying, close your eyes, and begin to repeat out loud or silently inside your head any rhythmical set of words that seems to match a natural, peaceful breathing pattern. Synchronize your breathing to the repetitions of the chant. Continue until you begin to feel peaceful and your breathing becomes regular. You can then stop the chanting and you should be able to retain the peaceful feeling for a number of hours, depending on what you are doing. The more peaceful you are before you began to chant, the easier it is to reach a deeply peaceful feeling. It is possible to have many hours of an uninterrupted peaceful feeling using a chant. While in this peaceful state, spiritual messaging is usually enhanced and reception made clearer. The noteworthy feature of a chant is that it works without the person having to significantly change his or her lifestyle. Modern medicine, in much the same manner, takes away pain using medication without having to change the lifestyle causing the pain.

Personal chanting works well for one person. Group chanting, on the other hand, can do the same thing for large groups of people all at one time. It is possible through a properly orchestrated sequence of music, chanting, singing, poetry, and prose readings (such as in a traditional church service) to create the same kind of peaceful feeling in a large group of people simultaneously that will last for hours and sometimes even for days.

HOW CAN I BRING MY BODY INTO BALANCE?

There are a number of methods or techniques available for bringing the human body into some kind of balance. The ones that seem to work particularly well for most Americans are (in alphabetical order): avoiding drugs, chanting, eating properly, mantras, massage, music, meditation, prayer, physical exercise, religious service, smells, and yoga. Each of these can balance the body for some period of time. For many people, chanting, mantras, meditation, prayer, and religious service last several hours. Avoiding drugs, eating properly, and physical exercise last for as long as the regimen is continued. The problem, if you can call it that, with avoiding drugs, eating properly, and physical exercise is that they often require a change in lifestyle. Chanting, mantras, meditation, prayer, and religious service require no real change in lifestyle—when they are done well they are very powerful and seem to work almost every time on a "come as you are" basis.

Practicing members of *Two* tend to focus, however, on avoiding drugs, eating properly, and physical exercise, taken together, because this combination can bring the body into steady balance over a long period of time. When the body is in balance, the clearest spiritual messages with the Two Sources are possible. The overall goal is to be in communication with *them* all day long about everything—no subject is too trivial or too complex.

How does meditation fit in?

Meditation in one form or another should be an important part of any adult life. It is even more important for practicing members of *Two*. The main purpose of meditation for the members of *Two* is to reestablish balanced blood flow in the body. Balanced blood flow means creating a condition where blood flows more or less symmetrically to both sides of the body. Restricting the flow of blood on one side of the body or the other appears to also restrict the clarity of spiritual messaging to One Source while increasing the clarity of spiritual messages to the Other Source. This is probably the source of the common political phrase "leaning to the left" or "leaning to the right," which invokes images of a person *physically* leaning to one side or the other and having a resultant political philosophy favoring the One Source or the Other Source.

Meditation for *Two* members, however, needs no fancy trappings. In its simplest form, here is all you need to do. Go to bed before you are dead tired, for most people usually around 8:30 or 9:00 P.M. Lie down in bed naked with a light blanket over you, on your back, toes pointed upward, no pillow, hands relaxed and at your sides, palms down. Breathe from the diaphragm and lungs simultaneously, moving your whole chest and abdomen up and down in sympathy to your heartbeat trying to use the up and down movement of your breathing to help move blood to all parts of your body. The main feature of this meditation technique is that, except for breathing, you *do not move*. Your body will think up all kinds of reasons why you should move, especially as you approach the "twenty-minute wall"—a hump that is difficult to get beyond. When you do get beyond the twenty-minute wall, however, it is fairly easy to hold still for thirty minutes or more. Typically, try to hold still for about 30—45 minutes.

Allow your body to think any thoughts or feel any feelings without restriction and without trying to guide them; the only rule is to not support the thought or feeling. Allow the thought or feeling to come up, reach whatever intensity it would like, and then fade away without comment or elaboration from your conscious processes. If anything, pretend to be an outside observer wondering what the subject of your next thought or feeling will be, in what order, with what intensity, and were these the same thoughts in the same sequence as last night. These are generally important spiritual messages that you will need to deal with, but not at this time. Please note that this kind of meditation is not intended to clear the mind of all thoughts and feelings, nor is it intended to stop thoughts and feelings. We certainly do not want to get in the habit of stopping thoughts and feelings because that would effectively close down spiritual communications. This is quite different from other religious that use meditation to actually try to "quiet the mind" or, to say it another way, to stop the spiritual messages.

Meditation time for *Two* members is primarily a "wind-down" time, a time to allow your body to slow down and to reestablish physical symmetry. Most people unknowingly restrict blood flow to parts of their body while they are performing certain activities during the day. A person tends to continue to hold these muscles tense even after they have finished the activity. The blood will gradually start to return to the tensed areas when you hold still at night, the process usually starting after 20—30 minutes of holding still. The first sign of blood returning to these starved areas is a kind of aching. Blood flow returning to the throat area may also produce the sensation to cough. Blood flow returning to the areas of the mouth, cheeks, or eyes will frequently cause salvia or tears to flow. Try not to swallow any more than absolutely necessary. The aching symptom seems to be the result of the nerves, which have also suffered from reduced blood flow, starting to wake up and return to normal. The first things the nerves want to report is that the tensed muscles are sore. The first tendency is to move, perhaps to roll over on your side, and continue to restrict the flow of blood to the affected area, thereby again cutting off the nerves' reports. Continuing to restrict the blood flow will make this pain go away but it is most likely an unwise strategy since long-term restriction of blood flow may cause future chronic problems. The pain reports that come from the nerves after about twenty minutes of holding still are the cause of the "twenty-minute wall" mentioned above. Occasionally, after the initial pain, a kind of tingling begins. The tingling is similar to what you feel when you have been sleeping on your arm and it has "fallen asleep" and you wake up and your arm begins to tingle as the blood rushes back. The tingling is followed by a feeling of rhythmic pulsing or throbbing. The time elapse from pain to throbbing for a particular area takes no more than several minutes. The throbbing reminds me of a cat or dog licking a wound; only this time it is the body "licking" itself where it hurts from the inside!

Control of the Throbbing.

People seem to have developed good control over the flow of blood in their bodies. Perhaps it is a survival mechanism; if we cut ourselves we can restrict the flow of blood to the wounded area to prevent bleeding to death. Try an experiment sometime when you have accidentally cut yourself by first allowing the cut area to throb and then, by tensing your inner muscles, stop the throbbing. The blood will flow profusely from the cut when you can feel the cut throbbing. The blood flow is minimal when you focus to tense inner muscles to stop the throbbing feeling. Certainly this ability to control throbbing and, thus, to control bleeding is a valuable skill. This skill, however, can lead to long-term problems if normal blood flow is not allowed to return. The holding-still meditation allows you to: (1) find those areas in your body that have reduced blood flow and allow these areas to return to normal blood flow; and (2) very importantly, re-learn what normal blood flow feels like in those areas of long-term restricted blood flow. You cannot successfully return an area of your body to all-day proper blood flow until you have re-learned what it feels like to have proper blood flow there and that feeling becomes "normal." Otherwise, whenever you let go of paying attention to the blood flow in a particular area of your body, that part will revert to whatever feels normal. Problems can result when the normal feeling is associated with restricted blood flow.

People frequently talk about tension in their body as an abstract mental or psychological concept and do not think to associate it with anything specifically physical in their body. Understand "tension" to be holding muscles "tense" or "tight" after the original need to tense the muscle has disappeared. The by-product of tension or holding a muscle tight is often an area of your body with reduced blood flow. If you strain your back lifting something and continue to hold the muscles tense in your lower back to prevent feeling the pain of the strain, your back will become sore—very sore. Only when you can relax the muscles to allow proper blood flow can you begin to heal your strained back.

Two things, however, are required to heal an injured area of the body: (1) proper blood flow to the area; and (2) proper nutrients in the blood to do the repair work once the blood is flowing properly.

Why does it seem to be difficult to lie flat on your back without moving? Something seems to be driving us to roll over. What is it? Restoring blood flow may seem like a fairly straightforward thing to do, but it is not. Some of the places of tension-induced restricted blood flow are for psychological reasons. Trying to return blood flow to these areas brings a flood of unexpected emotions. The following is an example reported recently by a person trying to use the holding-still meditation:

When I was in grade school we were required to say the Pledge of Allegiance to the American flag first thing each morning. We were required to hold our hand over our heart. We were told to place our open palm under our left breast— I assumed that was the location of my heart. My maternal grandfather died when I was eight years old of a heart attack. I assumed that a heart attack was literally "my heart attacking me," causing me to die. I did not hear anyone suggest that perhaps my grandfather's heart attack may have been caused by a high-fat diet and smoking cigarettes. I was afraid, in my eight-year-old mind, that I might have a heart attack at any moment. Thereafter, any time I felt a tinge of pain just underneath my left breast, where I thought my heart was located, I thought that I might be having a heart attack. I would then tense up the muscles on the left side of my chest.

Now fast forward forty years. I am an adult practicing my holding-still meditation, and I feel the blood starting to pulse into the left side of my chest. It is clear to me that I am holding muscles deep inside the left side of my chest tense, and I am frightened to let go. When I let the muscles relax a little and I begin to feel some pain, I feel as though I might die if I continue to relax these muscles. I cannot tell why I feel this way except that it is a very serious feeling of dread each time I relax the muscles and feel some pain in the exact area where I used to place my hand when I pledged allegiance to the flag in grade school. It took me several years of gradually relaxing these chest muscles little by little, checking it out carefully, and when nothing bad happened, relaxing them a little more, all the while trying to deal rationally with these feelings of impending death. It took quite some time to figure out all the inter-connections and it almost seems silly to tell the story now. Yet, these emotions and the resulting tension were very real.

DIETARY INFORMATION

WHAT ARE MOOD-ALTERING DRUGS?

A mood-altering drug is any drug that has the ability to alter your mood, such as a substance that can instantly change you from tired to energetic, from shy to talkative, from groggy to alert, or from inhibited to experimental. The common mood-altering drugs are alcohol, caffeine, cocoa, nicotine, and sugarcane. The mood-altering drugs work, in part, by changing the chemical balance of the body in some manner that is not sustainable over a long period of time. The one important side effect for practicing members of *Two* is that the mood-altering drugs tend to scramble the spiritual messages. The scrambling effect of mood-altering drugs gradually wears off in 48—72 hours.

Mood-altering drugs are very popular for a good reason: they are pleasant. Unfortunately, many people quickly become physiologically and/or emotionally addicted to these drugs. You can generally tell if you are addicted to a drug by asking these three simple questions:

(1) Can I go two weeks without using a particular drug?

(2) Does going without the drug cause me to have headaches, be irritable, or have trouble sleeping?

(3) Can I give or go to a party without using a particular drug?

Clearly, a particular drug will not have the same addictive qualities to all people.

Is sugarcane a mood-altering drug?

Why is sugarcane considered a mood-altering drug? After all, isn't sugar cane just sucrose? How is it different from other sucrose-containing substances, such as honey or maple syrup? There is no scientific evidence to understand why sugarcane is different from other sucrose-containing substances. Yet sugarcane is clearly addictive for some people while honey or maple syrup frequently is not.

The users of sugarcane products are willing to spend considerable money in a vending machine for something containing a few ounces of sugarcane but are not willing to spend the same money for a few ounces of honey or maple syrup. This probably also explains why we do not see carrots or broccoli in vending machines. It may be that it is not the sucrose in sugarcane that is mood-altering but rather some other substance either natural to cane or perhaps something that is part of the manufacturing process. Whatever it is, honey or maple syrup will not satisfy the cravings for sugarcane products.

WHAT IS THE "PLEASANT TOXIC EFFECT"?

People also enjoy another pleasant mood-altering experience that has come to be known as the "pleasant toxic effect." The effect upon the human body of ingesting a mildly toxic substance is feeling light-headed, dizzy, giddy. This is assuming that the ingested toxin is somewhat benign (has no immediate serious side effect, such as blindness), and the amount ingested is not sufficient to cause unconsciousness or death. The pleasant toxic effect accounts for part of the pleasure derived from alcoholic drinks; the toxin is in this case, of course, grain alcohol. However, it is also possible to re-create the pleasant toxic effect with other substances, such as mushrooms (the common toxin is sodium nitrate) and potato skins (the toxin is solanine). What should seem like the sheer terror of poisoning oneself often becomes expressed as laughter. There is no explanation for this phenomenon, except to say that being a human being is definitely a unique experience.

Other foods containing a toxin (such as zucchini, eggplant, and green tomatoes, which all contain the toxin solanine) were at one time in history considered too toxic to eat. Apparently, the willingness to ingest poison has varied from time to time. The pleasure can be intensified, to a point, by using several toxins at once, as in the case of alcohol and potato skins. Although there is a fine line for most people, ingest a little too much and a crushing headache will ensue.

Ingested toxins have the same basic effect as mood-altering drugs in that both tend to scramble spiritual messages and both require several days to return to normal.

IS IT EASY TO STOP USING MOOD-ALTERING DRUGS?

Coming off mood-altering drugs is not easy. Doing it all by yourself is even more difficult. During the first year off drugs, many people become energized by the thought of what they are doing. It is often great fun talking to other people about it. By the end of the first year, however, most people will not want to hear any more about it (particularly if they are still using the drugs)!

Then comes the second year. Something very strange often begins to happen during the second year off drugs. Your body will begin to change. You can feel it changing. Through the first year it will be almost as though your body is saying, "Look, we are not going to go through all the trouble to reconfigure if you are just going to start taking these drugs again in a few months." Somewhere near the beginning of the second year your body will begin to say, "Hey, you must be serious about this. We need to make some modifications if we are never going to get any more mood-altering drugs." Therefore, your body will begin to change. These changes feel as though they are deep-inside changes. You can feel them going on at night when you lie very still and quiet. It is a little scary. It is as though everything you have built up over the years, all the attributes that made you the person that you are, begins to melt away. You can feel them disappearing. You will start to become something else, something that you have not consciously planned. It is as though all of your life you have worn this heavy, wool, hooded robe that is your personality. Let us say that you generally like your personality; it is who you are or, at least, who you want to be. You know, in your heart of hearts, that you are naked underneath, but it does not matter because the robe so effectively covers you up from view. No one can see your naked self. Now, it feels as though you are standing up and the robe is starting to fall off in slow motion. Part of you will want to catch the robe as it slides off, but part of you will be curious to see what you look like naked; you have been covered up for such a long time.

For the first time in your life, your body will begin to take a new shape all by itself, moving down a path without your conscious direction. There will be moments when you will desperately want to try to hold it back from this change. You will be afraid that you will lose yourself. What you are becoming did not seem to be anything, just undefined. Year two is not for the faint-hearted!

WHAT ARE *TWO'S* GENERAL DIETARY RECOMMENDATIONS?

The most effective strategy for improving the clarity of spiritual messaging is avoiding mood-altering drugs. Clarity generally improves each time a person eliminates another mood-altering drug. The second most effective strategy is eating the proper foods to bring the body into a chemical balance.

The human body is more or less a big chemical factory that works best when the body chemistry is in balance (neither too much nor too little of any given nutrient/chemical). The food a person eats affects, to a large degree but not exclusively, the chemical balance. Of the many different possible diet regimens promoted today in popular American culture, *Two* needed to find a dietary recommendation for members that would be safe and beneficial from a health point of view and effective from a spiritual point of view. Here are the basic concepts recommended at this time by *Two*

Over the years, various diets, food philosophies, and personal eating testimonies were studied in detail by members, and some were tried for their effectiveness for spiritual messaging. Eventually, any diet recommendations that had been started and promoted by a living individual were suspect and ultimately rejected because one lifetime seemed like an insufficient testing period. Rejected also were any diets that had not had extensive scientific scrutiny. In the end, it was not possible to find any one particular diet containing specific combinations of foods that seemed suitable, that we would be willing to bet our life and health on.

The Dietary Goal.

It was decided to select foods to be eaten on the basis of their nutritional content measured against some standard nutritional goals rather than choose a particular diet type that would specify foods to be or not to be eaten. The National Academy of Sciences Recommended Dietary Allowance (the current edition—as of this writing the tenth edition) was selected as the standard base-line for nutrient intake requirements for a normal healthy individual. Called the United States Recommended Dietary Allowances (USRDA), these recommendations are designed only *to prevent a deficiency* and may not necessarily optimize other dietary or health-related goals. There may be reasons to take some nutrients in larger doses, such as using high doses of Vitamin C and Vitamin A to help fight an infection. These larger doses should be considered "therapeutic" doses rather than day-to-day "maintenance" doses. Therapeutic doses of any nutrient should be done with great care and probably under the advice of a registered dietitian.

It becomes immediately obvious that in order to follow the USRDA a person must eat a wide variety of foods. A computer is almost a necessity to sum up daily the thirty or more nutrients for each food eaten. (See the New American Religion Web site *www.NewAmericanReligion.org* for more information on computer-aided nutrient analysis.) The goal is to try to fall within 75—200 percent of the USRDA for the age, sex, body type, activity level, and reproductive factors of an individual. Almost any nontoxic food, not containing mood-altering substances, in almost any amount is allowed as long as total nutrient intake falls within 75—200 percent of the USRDA guidelines.

WHY IS 75—200 PERCENT OF USRDA THE RECOMMENDED NUTRIENT AMOUNTS?

Trying to achieve *exactly* a diet of the USRDA recommended nutrients is impossible. Trying to hit within a range of 75—125 percent may sound reasonable but it, too, is almost impossible for an ordinary American. Enlarging the target range to 75—200 percent, is still difficult but is possible in normal daily life. It is important to be reasonable with these kinds of goals in order not to become frustrated or unnecessarily compulsive. Also, keep in mind the accuracy with which people measure the amount of foods eaten. For example, a person can reasonably measure the amount of orange juice they drink as a quarter, half, or full 8-ounce glass. However, most people cannot really tell the difference between ¼ and ³/₈ of a glass. Therefore, the measuring tolerance should be no tighter than ± 25 percent.

It therefore seems reasonable to set target goals at a tolerance equal to or greater than measuring tolerance. Also, keep in mind that when a computer says, for example, that you have eaten 65.3 grams of protein in a given day, it is an unreliably accurate-looking number. Since measuring tolerance is generally about ± 25 percent, it is correct to interpret the computer output of 65.3 grams as closer to 65.3 grams ± 25 percent—meaning that a person has probably eaten somewhere between 48 grams (.75 * 65.3) and 82 grams (1.25 * 65.3) of protein.

ARE THERE FOODS THAT SHOULD BE AVOIDED?

In general, avoid any foods that send your body into either a frenzy or lethargy or will poison your body. Your body will, as much as possible, prioritize body activity and functions based upon the necessity to do them. If you disrupt body chemistry, with a poison for example, the body will shift into action to eliminate the poison on a fairly high-priority basis. During such time, things like spiritual communication are given a low priority. Clear spiritual communication depends greatly on a body in good condition with no distracting high-priority functions consuming available resources. The following are some examples of trying to put into practice the above general recommendations:

- Avoid any food that contain or have been prepared with mood-altering drugs (such as sugarcane, molasses, sorghum, cocoa, caffeine, and alcohol).
- Avoid frequent use of herbal teas that have mood-altering effects.
- Avoid foods that contain excessive amounts of toxins (for example, mushrooms contain the toxin sodium nitrate; potato skins, zucchini, eggplant, and green

tomatoes contain the toxin solanine; Spanish peanuts, and walnuts may contain aflatoxins).

For people who enjoy peanuts or peanut butter, it should be noted that Valencia peanuts are not susceptible to and, therefore, do not contain aflatoxins.

- Avoid toxic food additives such as preservatives; carcinogenic substances, such as caramel coloring; and any other known harmful substance.
- Avoid heavy use of foods that are irritants to the eyes or mucus membranes (onions, garlic, black pepper, and leeks).
- Avoid heavily spiced foods that cause perspiration, watering eyes, running nose or a burning sensation in the mouth.

WHAT ARE SOME USEFUL RECOMMENDATIONS REGARDING FOOD AND FOOD PREPARATION?

1. Eat five or six meals per day—the three standard meals plus a mid-morning and mid-afternoon snack and sometimes an evening snack. Do not eat anything within three hours of going to sleep since it will tend to interfere with sleep.

2. Drink a glass of water before each of the three main meals, drink water or juice with meals, and sip water all day long while working. If possible, use a computer to calculate the amount of water in the foods you have eaten and add this amount to the total amount of water you drink during the day to calculate the total amount of water consumed in a day. In general, try to achieve a total of about five to eight 8-ounce glasses of water per day.

3. Drink filtered water and try to avoid water with significant chlorine, fluoride, toxic, or carcinogenic contaminates.

4. Use drinks such as carbonated waters and juices or hot milk and honey for special occasions. Do not drink alcohol because alcohol is a poison and seriously addictive to many people. Gain the

benefits of drinking red wine by drinking grape juice or, even better, eating fresh red grapes.

5. Eat primarily whole-grain breads.
6. Shop at least once each week to eat foods that are as fresh as possible.
7. Try to eat 75 percent or more of foods that have been grown organically. The idea of fewer chemicals and more sustainable agriculture seems good.
8. Most of the food should be steamed or boiled to avoid damaging or changing the chemicals in food. Avoid the use of a microwave oven and standard convection oven because the high temperatures may destroy micronutrients and/or living things in the food.
9. Try to eat some raw foods every day.
10. Modify fiber intake until your feces have a fluffy, almost floating look (rather than a compact, sinking-to-bottom-of-the-bowl look).

Note that there are no specific restrictions on meats. Various meats have many nutritional benefits. The understanding of human nutritional needs is insufficient at this time to consider a total abstention from meats. If meals are planned following the USRDA nutritional guidelines, it will automatically restrict the amount of meat allowed in the diet. A growing number of people have difficulty eating meats for various reasons (such as, concern for earth's ecology, cruelty to animals, taste or aesthetic considerations, and the lethargic feeling often accompanying the ingestion of a large amount of meat). What we can say at this time is that meats used sparingly as condiments do not seem to interfere with spiritual messaging.

Why eat many different kinds of foods?

Each food generally has one or two, or possibly several, nutrients in abundance, while the rest of the nutrients are in much smaller quantities. Therefore, it is necessary to eat many different kinds of foods each day to achieve a balanced diet. Even so, it is difficult to eat a wide enough variety of foods in a single day to obtain a balanced diet. Therefore, it is probably a good idea to allow yourself to average nutrients over a week's time.

People are usually tired when they get home from a full day at work. Frequently they are in no mood to slice eight or ten different vegetables for dinner. In addition, it is hard to cook in small quantities, such as for one or two people, when using many different kinds of foods in one recipe. A good solution to this problem is to slice eight or ten different vegetables in a larger quantity once a week, steam them with some rice, and store the leftovers together. Use the leftover rice and vegetables as a base for cooking many different recipes (soups, stews, pasta sauces, creamed entries, omelets). This makes meal preparation much faster and the ability to obtain a wide variety of nutrients much easier. See the New American Religion Web site, *www.NewAmericanReligion.org*, for specific details on the rice and vegetable recipe and other recipes.

WHAT ABOUT NUTRIENT SUPPLEMENTS?

Should a person use vitamin/nutrient supplements? The answer is "yes," but only for a limited time to solve a special problem until you can figure out how to get the nutrient from foods. A supplement should not be considered as good a source of a nutrient as obtaining the nutrient from a food. If you do use a supplement, take only the supplemental nutrient you actually need, rather than taking something like a multivitamin, especially if the multivitamin provides close to 100 percent of the daily requirements. Obviously, the multivitamin taken in conjunction with your normal food intake may well push the percent of the daily amounts of a nutrient above 200 percent. Consider a supplement undesirable if it throws the body chemistry out of balance (by supplying more than 200 percent of the USRDA). Having too much of a nutrient may be as bad as having too little of a nutrient, especially if you are striving for a chemical balance.

Here is another reason to be hesitant about a supplement. A particular chemical/nutrient, say Vitamin C (ascorbic acid), in a food is accompanied by other chemicals adjoining ascorbic acid. Some chemicals that adjoin a nutrient may be equally important for things like making the exact or pure chemical easier for a body to handle. The human body may, in fact, need the whole array of chemicals adjoining a particular nutrient to satisfy what appears in charts as a single chemical. Think about a single chemical/nutrient, such as ascorbic acid, as only a marker to help identify certain kinds of foods containing the group of chemicals you need rather than thinking that you only need the single, pure chemical.

How does this diet affect appetite?

One of the most interesting side affects about eating in this manner and avoiding mood-altering drugs is the loss of the traditional "appetite." It is not uncommon for a mother to say to her child, "Don't eat sweets before dinner, it will ruin your appetite." Often one's appetite is closer in reality to being a mood-altering drug "craving" (perhaps even addiction). What would happen to a person's "appetite" if they had no mood-altering drug cravings? The old feelings that are often identified with appetite disappear. Moreover, it is not replaced with anything nearly as dramatic. Instead, hunger is experienced as a feeling of weakness or loss of energy sometimes accompanied with an empty feeling in the stomach. Although the empty feeling in the stomach is not very strong and will seem to go away if a person does not pay attention to it, the weakness, due to lack of food, does not go away. The weakness gradually increases until it becomes indistinguishable from tiredness. It is possible to postpone eating for a number of hours, but five or six active hours seems to be the upper comfortable limit.

MISCELLANEOUS

WHAT ARE THE SEXUAL IMPLICATIONS OF THIS RELIGION?

As a person begins to bring his or her body into balance and begins to live the idea of two equal Sources, it is not uncommon for sexual attitudes to also begin to change. A natural by-product of bringing your body into balance is often a growing awareness and sensitivity to both the male and female parts of your body and the male and female components of your mental and emotional makeup. The expanding awareness and sensitivity has resulted in some changes in sexual attitudes. Here is an excerpt of one member's experience.

Most of my earlier heterosexual experiences involved using the standard "missionary position" (that is, the woman on her back, legs spread apart, man face down and on top), or the "reverse missionary position" (that is, man on bottom, legs together, woman on top straddling the male). The standard or reverse missionary positions seem to me to be consistent with the patriarchal religions because the missionary positions:
(1) Promote a quick male ejaculation;

(2) Allow for deep penetration into the female, increasing the chance of pregnancy;

(3) Make manipulation by our hands of our genitals during the sexual encounter very difficult; and

(4) Appear to offer little long-term satisfaction for the female.

These features seemed consistent with a male-dominated religion that did not want to sanction sexual pleasure outside of procreation or promote the sexual satisfaction of the female.

Recently, however, I have found myself replacing the missionary position with the "T" position: woman on her back, legs spread apart, a right-handed male lying on the right-hand side of the female, on his left side perpendicular to the woman, the woman's right leg over the top of the male's body, the female's left leg between the male's legs. I think of it as the "T" position because the two bodies more or less form the position of the letter "T," with the man's body as the top of the "T" and the women as the upright. The "T" position allows each person to use his or her own hands to promote and control the level of stimulation so that the male does not climax before the female and the male has better control over his erection. Both the male and the female now have the possibility of using their hands to increase stimulation of the female. One way the male can increase stimulation of the female is by rhythmically alternating back and forth from a shallow penetration in the vagina to removing the penis entirely from the vagina and using the penis head to gently massage the entire genital area of the female.

The increased friction around the female genital area requires careful attention to be sure that the vagina, outer lips (labia), and clitoris of the female is moist and well-lubricated. This can be accomplished easily by either moving the lubricating juices from the vagina outward with the fingers or by applying saliva or synthetic lubricants to the female genital areas. A major advantage of the "T" position is the possibility to extend the period of active sexual contact considerably since the male can massage the female genital area and gain shallow penetration to a well-lubricated vagina with or without an erection. If an erection is lost, it can usually be regained through self-manipulation as required or, in the absence of a male erection, pleasurable sexual contact for both the male and female can continue without a male erection. A female can rightfully expect, regardless, that the man will not withdraw from the "T" position until she is ready for him to separate from her.

WHAT DOES IT MEAN TO BE A "FRIEND TO YOUR BODY"?

While trying to increase the clarity of the spiritual messages, think about trying to develop a new friendship with your body. Consider taking the attitude that you and your body are a team, a good team, and that there are probably many things you could do to help your body perform its functions. Let the idea of working together with your body for common purposes grow in your mind. Look at the things your body has to do and ask yourself, "How can I help?" Here a is reported example.

An important feature of working with my body through-out the day is trying to learn to hold my body in a symmet-rical position. Although I am hesitant to admit it, I think this might be similar to what my grandmother meant when she said, "sit up straight." I consider my body to be in an asymmetrical position if I cross my legs or lean to one side while sitting or drape my arm over the back of a chair. This causes my heart to have to work harder to get blood to the side of my body that I am leaning on or to get blood to the leg I have crossed. My body would seem to prefer if I hold myself in a position where any restriction of blood flow is more or less uniform on both sides of my body. I try also to keep my body in a symmetrical position when walking, running, or swimming. When I am walking, I try to carry any loads in a backpack with the straps over each shoulder so as to try to not only balance the load but also prevent the load from causing me to lean while walking. If I am leaning to one side or the other while walking, I am concerned that I will put an excessive and unnatural force on my hip, knee and ankle joints, and also on my spine. Perhaps, over a period of time, I may even cause uneven wear to those bones and joints. I no longer carry my billfold in my rear pocket because of the effect of the billfold bulge on my sitting posture.

My body responds to all of this special attention by returning a pleasant or content feeling to me. It is very nice. One of the joys of this life-style (avoiding drugs and treating my body properly) is what is "missing." Here is a list of my missing life events:

__Headaches:__ I have not had a headache in fifteen years and I used to have terrific three aspirin headaches several times a week.

__Diarrhea or Constipation:__ My feces were frequently either uncomfortably too runny or too firm; now my bowel movements are regular, and my feces are soft to fluffy.

__Night Blindness:__ It was not uncommon to walk into a movie theater and not be able to see; now my night vision is normal.

__Depression:__ I saw a psychologist, social worker, or psychiatrist mostly for depression for a few months every year for

*the ten years preceding eating properly and avoiding drugs.
I am no longer bothered by depression.*

*Insomnia: Insomnia had been a problem for me my
entire adult life. I now sleep peacefully with gentle dreams
and if I am awakened in the middle of the night, I fall back
to sleep easily.*

*Frequent colds: It was not uncommon for me to have three
to five colds per year; now I have less than one cold per year.*

*Bad decisions: Because my head is clearer, I make better
decisions for myself, which makes my overall living experience a lot nicer.*

*Temper: In the past, it was not difficult to make me
angry or for me to lose my temper; now it stills happens occasionally but very infrequently.*

*Loneliness: It was easy for me to feel lonely in a crowd of
people. It is not that loneliness has now disappeared. (I still
need other people to make my life complete and I still feel some
loneliness at times.) Rather what has now disappeared is the
frantic feeling that accompanied the feelings of loneliness.*

*Impatience: I have been very impatient all my life. The
last fifteen years, however, has been the first time that I have
been able to slow down and begin to savor life events. Part
of my new-found patience is probably due to just growing
older but another part seems to be due to not taking stimu-
lants and being more rested.*

*If someone had enumerated the above list to me when I
was young, I doubt that it would have been sufficient for me
to give up caffeine, alcohol, cocoa, nicotine, and sugarcane*

and try to lead a balanced life. I would have felt that life was not worth living without my mood-altering drugs. If I could have achieved the same results by giving up celery, I would have done it in a minute.

One other experience may be worth relating. While camping one day in late August, a butterfly flew into my tent, became trapped, and could not find its way out. I went over to the butterfly and, by forming images in my gut and words in my mind, offered to take the butterfly out of the tent if it would land on my hand. I held my right hand out in front of me with my index finger extended. The butterfly flew immediately to my hand. I wondered how I could carry the butterfly across the large tent. I thought it would be best if I cupped my left hand over the butterfly. I tried to do so. The butterfly let me know that it was afraid that I would damage its wings and flew off several feet. Renegotiating and promising to leave my left hand at my side, I extended my right hand again. The butterfly again flew over and perched on my index finger. I carried it across the tent to the opening. I was deeply touched by the wonderful moment of having the butterfly on my finger. I am very pleased such communication is possible. I feel blessed to now have these kinds of contacts with the life around me.

WHY NINETEEN YEARS?

Why are summary publications scheduled on a nineteen-year cycle; why nineteen and not twenty or twenty-four or whatever? In order to answer that question, a brief discussion about astronomy is required.

Earth/Moon System:

First, the earth does *not* rotate around the center of the sun, and the moon does *not* rotate around the center of earth. Rather the earth and the moon are a system that rotates about a central point that lies part way between the earth's axis and the moon's axis. It is the center point of the earth/moon system that follows an orbital path about the center point of our solar/matter system. The center point of our solar/matter system is near but not exactly the same as the center of the sun.

Meanwhile, the earth and the moon are in a beautiful dance, weaving in and out about the earth/moon center point as the center point of the earth/moon travels along the orbital path. Sometimes part of the earth is moving forward in orbit in the same direction as the earth/moon center point (such as during the new moon). Sometimes the earth is moving backwards in orbit in the opposite direction of the earth/moon system center point (such as during the full moon). It is these changes in the motion of earth due to the earth/moon system that are, in part, the reason why many of us feel differently at different phases of the moon. It is not the phase of the moon that creates the feelings, it is the change in direction and change in net orbital velocity of earth. The phase of the moon may be thought of only as a marker indicating to us the nature of earth's present motion. Our bodies are very sensitive to these motion changes as we ride along on the moving surface of earth. Much more sensitive than we currently recognize.

Now imagine the position of the earth/moon system in relationship to the sun on the vernal equinox on or about March 21st. Let us further imagine that sun, moon, and earth are all aligned in that order in a straight line on March 21st, indicating a new moon. Next year, we all know, that on March 21st there will not be a new moon. To say it another way, the cycle of the earth/moon system (roughly 29 ½ days) will not work out to be an exactly even number of cycles in a given year. The question might be asked, "How many years, if ever, will it take for another new moon to occur on March 21st?" The answer is nineteen years. Every nineteen years the sun, moon, and earth will all be in the same relative position. That means that every nineteen years humans will feel the exact same repetition of moving due to the earth/moon system at the exact same times of the year!

The nineteen-year cycle:

The nineteen-year cycle is a very important, albeit not commonly recognized, cycle in human life. Important events often occur, or reoccur in slightly different forms, at the nineteen-year sequence in a person's life. For example, in American society a nineteen-year old person has normally graduated from high school and is starting college or starting an adult life, much like being born and having to learn a new way of life. A thirty-eight-year old person will often begin a new job or have a major life change. The same is true for a fifty-seven-year old person. We tend to start each of these cycles with similar kinds of events, and often we will move through the nineteen-year cycle in a remarkably similar repetition of the earlier cycle with only the details of the specific events changing.

If you would like to have an interesting experience sometime, select one photo that is representative of your life events for a particular year in your life. Arrange the first nineteen photos covering the first nineteen years of your life in a horizontal line. Next, arrange the photos covering age twenty to thirty-eight years directly alongside the photos for the first nineteen years of your life. Now arrange a third line of photos covering age thirty-nine to fifty-seven. Do you see a similar pattern in your nineteen-year cycles? Most people do.

The first nineteen years of human life will frequently set the pattern for each following nineteen-year life experience. Unfortunately, the nineteen-year cycle is long enough that it is difficult to recognize consciously the repetitiousness of it all without using some memory-enhancing technique such as laying out photographs. Nevertheless, we subconsciously feel that our life is following some kind of a pattern. The repetitious nineteen-year pattern is, perhaps, the source of the notion of "karma." Karma expresses the idea that something you did in the past influences what will happen to you in the future. The ordinary context for karma is usually related to previous lives; that idea is vaguely comprehensible to most members of *Two* through the recycling process of the light and matter from our current body into other male and female bodies. The recycled light and matter influence on our life, however, is probably pale in comparison with the influence of the first nineteen-year cycle. Can a person break out of these nineteen-year repetitive cycles? Probably, but only with great difficulty. Therefore, we are each at some point in our nineteen-year cycle that will repeat again in the next nineteen years. This year will feel vaguely familiar, depending on your age, to a year experienced nineteen, thirty-eight, fifty-seven or seventy-six years ago. Because of the nineteen-year cycles, we are able to place events stretching over the past nineteen years in a unique personal context. It is to honor the nineteen-year cycle that we have set the summary publications dates for *Two* (see Preferred Practice #9).

Most Americans do not understand or even know about the nineteen-year cycle. How could a well-educated person achieve adulthood and not know such an important piece of information? The reason, in part, is that we have a calendar that was created by men who were culturally influence by the Arab-based religions which honored only the One Source they call "Him." It is not surprising that our calendar is based only upon earth's imagined travel around the sun and that we relegate the moon to a body that circles around the earth. The sun is predominately a male icon; have you ever heard of the sun referred to as "Mother Sun?" If the calendar inventors had been influenced by a religion that honored both the male and the female, perhaps we would have a calendar that incorporates symbols for both the male and the female. Such a calendar might, for example, reference information about the sun and the moon and the nineteen-year cycle.

WHAT IS THE SOURCE OF EVIL?

The answer, of course, is that we are the source of evil. Alternatively, to say it another way, the Two Sources are the fundamental source of evil, that is, each Source contains the capacity for evil. Is there one single source of evil? Perhaps One Source is really the source of all evil and the Other Source is the source of all good? That does not seem likely; that would be like saying males are the source of all evil and females are the source of all good or, conversely, females are the source of all evil and males are the source of all good! While that idea might find sympathy in some foreign countries, I do not think that idea is going to fly in America. No, the capacity for evil is inherent in each Source. This becomes evident repeatedly when people communicate only with one of the Sources and begin acting only with reference to that single Source without fair and equal consideration for the other Source.

To put it in a political context, evil is at the extreme political left (for example, Stalin's brand of communism) or at the extreme political right (for example, Hitler's brand of fascism). Common experience confirms that evil tends to develop whenever a group gets too far to the left or to the right. Politically, the good might be said to be in the middle.

Good and evil, therefore, are not polar extremes with good at one side and evil at the other. Rather, evil dwells at the extremes and good dwells in the middle, with an equal balance of the Two Sources. In fact, in common American language, the word *unbalanced* is often used in place of the word *evil*. The "good" might in some sense also be said to coincide with "fairness," where both Sources are equally and fairly respected and represented with neither one dominating the other.

A huge source of personal confusion and a possible secondary source of evil acts ("God told me to do it" kind of thing) is the "Alice in Wonderland reversing effect"—a most curious human phenomenon. Consider, for example, when your gut feelings are telling you to do one thing and the voice inside your head is telling you to do something else. Which is correct?

Suppose you received a spiritual message as a gut feeling. If you are the kind of person that does not trust or are unable to act upon gut feelings, you may try to shift the "gut feeling" communication into "quiet voice words." The process of shifting a gut feeling to quiet voice words, however, reverses the content of the communication. If a spiritual message starts out as a gut feeling that is trying to tell you *to do* something it will come out as "quiet voice words" telling you *not to do* it. This is the source of the common human complaint where a person *feels* one way but the voice in their head is telling them the opposite. The same "Alice in Wonderland reversing effect" is true if a person tries to convert "quiet voice words" into "gut feelings."

People frequently use spiritual messages and the "Alice in Wonderland reversing effect" to develop a pro and con dialogue within themselves to weigh the various merits of a particular decision. While using this phenomenon in this manner is an interesting and perhaps useful exercise, it is a trivial use of spiritual messages. Learning to communicate with each of the Two Sources, around you and within your body, simultaneously in the natural language of each Source ("gut feelings" and "quiet voice words") without conversion is a much more powerful and direct tool for guiding personal behavior and decision making. Learning to do so, however, requires skill, practice, a certain reservoir of accumulated life experiences from which to draw, and a balance of communications from each Source.

The Twelve Preferred Practices

©

INTRODUCTION

Two: The New American Religion has functioned so far under some "preferred practices". These preferred practices have helped guide the development of the religion as it progresses and is refined, and protect the religion from being taken over by special interests or charismatic personalities.

Here is the checklist we have used:.

(1) Is the religion led by a charismatic person? [ ] yes [ ] no

(2) Does it deal with social or political issues? [ ] yes [ ] no

(3) Is there a large congregation of people? [ ] yes [ ] no

(4) Does it have religious buildings or property? [ ] yes [ ] no

(5) Is spiritual knowledge advanced by a holy person? [ ] yes [ ] no

(6) Is it male or female dominated? [ ] yes [ ] no

(7) Does it seek to convert anyone? [ ] yes [ ] no

(8) Does it ask for money? [ ] yes [ ] no

(9) Is it based upon divinely inspired written material? [ ] yes [ ] no

(10) Is spiritual information verbally delivered to large groups? [ ] yes [ ] no

(11) Does it require a public ritual? [ ] yes [ ] no

(12) Is it a large organization? [ ] yes [ ] no

If the answer to any of these questions is "yes," we feel we are not remaining true to our original vision.

Preferred Practice #1: Two is to be a religion based upon spiritual discoveries made by many individual people working together and not by a single, charismatic personality.

From time to time a human being with an impressive spiritual demeanor, someone appearing to be "holy" or "saintly," will appear who is beguilingly charismatic and has the ability to accumulate followers, apostles, devotees, or converts. Such a person is to be welcomed as an ordinary member of *Two* but is to have no unusual or predominate role, because the spiritual experiences of any one person are too narrow.

Two should be a religion that grows and evolves from the efforts of many people over time. The summary input of many people's experiences over a long period of time will best represent the complexity of the spiritual realms. *Two* should be a religion that is based on an accumulating body of spiritual information that is constantly updated by ordinary people and refined by individual experiences and discoveries. *Two* should be, like any other theory, subject to common scrutiny with the clear and absolute understanding that there will never be a single person with "divine insight" for this new religion.

PREFERRED PRACTICE #2: TWO IS TO BE A RELIGION WHOSE FOCUS IS ENTIRELY SPIRITUAL AND NOT SOCIAL OR POLITICAL.

There are many social and political problems in the world needing immediate attention, and it is a good thing that people form organizations to deal with those problems. However, *Two* is to be a religion that focuses entirely upon spiritual matters, and not on social, political, ecological, or any other non-spiritual issues.

PREFERRED PRACTICE #3: TWO IS TO BE A RELIGION THAT FOCUSES ON THE INDIVIDUAL PERSON AND NOT ON A LARGE CONGREGATION OF PEOPLE.

Two is a religion that disseminates and discusses spiritual information on a one-person to one-person basis. The one-to-one sharing of information on the Web or in person is to be the hallmark of this religion. Spiritual information must, out of necessity, be more generalized as the size of the discussion group grows.

Living Room Gatherings.

Two realizes, however, that some people will benefit by participating in virtual or live groups. In such cases, the basic group should be kept small in size, and the focus should be on the spiritual success of each person within the group and not the success of the group. The basic gathering size of any such virtual or live group should be the size that can comfortably gather in an ordinary living room in a typical member's home with the maximum size of no more than ten to twelve adult people (the group is to be called a *Living Room Gathering*). The Living Room Gathering will help prevent any one individual or any small group of people from taking control of the religion. The purpose of the Living Room Gathering is to:

(1) Provide support for each other in the personal process of learning how to more clearly send and receive spiritual messages;
(2) Discuss personal spiritual experiences;
(3) Pass on valuable learned lessons and exchange information;
(4) Celebrate beauty;
(5) Share information on, and when possible eat, healthful foods together; and
(6) Share information on exercising the body and mind.

If regular meetings are desired, Living Room Gatherings should meet sometime between the first Friday evening and the first Sunday evening after the occurrence of a full moon. Relating the Living Room Gathering to the lunar cycle will help the members keep track of the lunar cycle and better understand the changes in their mind and body during the different phases of the lunar cycle.

Information about the participating members in a Living Room Gathering, as well as information in general about the members of *Two*, is not to be public.

PREFERRED PRACTICE #4: TWO IS TO BE A RELIGION THAT SHARES SPIRITUAL INFORMATION ON THE WEB, THROUGH EMAIL, OR WHERE PEOPLE NORMALLY MEET IN ORDINARY LIFE, AND NOT IN A RELIGIOUS BUILDING.

A religious building has the ability to capture a specific spiritual feeling that was determined when the building was designed and built. *Two* does not want to meet in a building that has a "specific spiritual feeling" to it. When Living Room Gatherings occur, let the meeting place be in various familiar settings or comfortable on-line chat spaces or in one of the member's home (a different location for each meeting wherever possible). The spiritual feeling presented by familiar settings will be more current and more reflective of the members' personal lives.

Large Quarterly Gatherings.

Some Living Room Gatherings will want to get together with other Living Room Gatherings, and *Two* does not want to eliminate all group activity larger than the size of the Living Room Gatherings. There are important functions that are possible in a larger group. The exchange of information among a larger group has definite advantages. Therefore, if it is desired, let this kind of exchange of information occur at a larger scale in the following manner.

The Living Room Gatherings may decide to come together in a larger regional group composed of several, or even many, Living Room Gatherings. These regional gatherings should occur on the first weekend following the occurrence of the spring equinox, summer solstice, autumnal equinox, or winter solstice. These gatherings should be held on-line and/or in a beautiful setting not owned by the religion. The cost of the outdoor gatherings should be kept to a minimum. Beauty is the signature of the Two Sources. Therefore, the Large Quarterly Gatherings should be a time of general celebration of beauty by all members and their families (whether or not they are participating in the larger formal gatherings). The purpose of the larger gatherings is similar to the local gatherings but allow for things that are only possible at a larger scale and to include a special celebration of the following.

Vernal Equinox   Children, New Birth, and Freedom
(approx. March 21st) Over Absolute Death

Summer Solstice   Human Freedom
(approx. June 21st)

Autumnal Equinox   O.T.H.E.R. celebration
(approx. September 21st) (OtherThan Human Earth
                          Relatives celebration in honor
                          of all the other nonhuman
                          forms of life that enrich
                          human life)

Winter Solstice   The Two Sources
(approx. December 21st)

See the New American Religion Web site *www.NewAmericanReligion.org* for the date and location of upcoming Large Quarterly Gatherings.

PREFERRED PRACTICE #5: SPIRITUAL KNOWLEDGE IS TO BE ADVANCED BY MANY ORDINARY PEOPLE THROUGH THE MODERN ORAL TRADITION AND NOT BY RELIGIOUS LEADERS (SUCH AS PRIESTS, MINISTERS, RABBIS OR ANY OTHER SELF-PROCLAIMED RELIGIOUS LEADER).

A religious leader can only accurately represent his or her own personal religious experience. *Two* needs to incorporate much broader religious experiences, the kind of experiences that only a group of people can represent. A religious leader, for those very few occasions when a leader is required for some specific purpose, should not be a regularly ordained or stationed person. Rather, the role should be fulfilled by an individual temporarily stepping into the position and should be done on a rotating basis with other people to represent the broadest possible religious experiences.

(See Preferred Practice #9 for more information on the modern oral tradition.)

PREFERRED PRACTICE #6: TWO IS TO BE NEITHER MALE NOR FEMALE DOMINATED.

Two strives to be a friendly religion, neither snobbish nor authoritarian in demeanor and neither male nor female dominated. *Two* should be open and friendly to all people. If members do not represent the ethnic and gender mix of the surrounding society, something is wrong.

PREFERRED PRACTICE #7: TWO IS TO BE A RELIGION THAT RESPECTS THE BELIEFS OF OTHERS AND DOES NOT SEEK TO CONVERT PEOPLE.

Information about *Two* should *not* be presented to anyone unless they first ask. If a person is happy with a particular religion it means that the metaphors of that religion are compatible with his or her life. Nothing more needs to be done. Until a person asks a question, no answers need to be offered. People who are willing to talk about *Two* can be recognized by their visible display of the *Two* image. No other announcement needs to be made. Many people will have no need of any religion whatsoever, and that is how it should be. The exception to this general practice has been the public advertising of the address location of the New American Religion Web site.

Preferred Practice #8: Two is to be a religion that does not collect money.

No one should ever be asked to donate money to *Two*. Once money is collected, a religion will often become dependent on the money. Let there be some spiritual practice that can stay forever focused on the spiritual realms without compromise. We have no need to grow, no need to be organized, no need to be efficient, no need to gain the benefits of scale, no reason to hurry, and no need for anything that will require the collection of money.

PREFERRED PRACTICE #9: TWO IS TO BE A RELIGION THAT DEPENDS ON CONSTANTLY CHANGING STORIES TO KEEP IT ALIVE AND VITAL.

Two has been a religion that is based on the "modern oral tradition," that is, direct communication from one person to another person primarily face to face (the oral tradition) but also online through the Web, telephone, and email (adding a modern extension to the old oral tradition). The information about the *Two* religion will be slightly changed each time the story is retold from one person to another person. Each time it is told and slightly changed, the new adaptation of the story will more closely fit the teller and the listener.

Hard copy, published information is too static, unchanging, and easily becomes archaic and ritualized. Hard copy, published information, while not suitable for everyday transfer of information, is on the other hand, ideally suited to maintaining a historical summary record of what has been discovered at each step along the path. Depend on the person-to-person modern oral tradition of dissemination to keep the religion alive and constantly changing and responsive to individual needs. Depend on the published summary, hard copy materials

to record the steps of the spiritual journey over time—
its progress, its backward steps, its awkward steps, its
detours. Because published spiritual information is too
easily used by charismatic personalities to promote
themselves and possibly plunge the religion into a personality cult, *all written information for this religion
must be published anonymously and only once every nineteen years.* It is proper that the authors should collect
royalties from their work, but if the authors choose to
identify themselves with their writing, assume the
information to be inauthentic and to be disregarded
and not part of this religion.

The first nineteen-year cycle summary publications,
of which this is one, will appear in the year 2000. The
second nineteen-year publication year will be in 2019.
Anyone can publish a summary book that records a full
nineteen-year-cycle of experiences. Any summary materials published outside of the nineteen-year-cycle year
will automatically be considered inauthentic and will be
disregarded and not part of this religion.

PREFERRED PRACTICE #10: THE VERBAL TRANSFER OF INFORMATION ABOUT TWO SHOULD, WHENEVER POSSIBLE, BE FROM ONE PERSON TO ANOTHER PERSON.

If information is delivered verbally to more than one person at a time, the group size should always be smaller than twenty-four people; otherwise the religion will be at risk for possibly developing into a personality cult based on a charismatic speaker.

PREFERRED PRACTICE #11: TWO IS TO BE A RELIGION THAT CAN BE PRACTICED FULLY AND COMPLETELY BY ONESELF, WITHOUT ANY PUBLIC RITUALS.

Many Americans consider spiritual practices and beliefs to be personal and are uncomfortable with public rituals or other displays of personal spiritual beliefs. The following are examples of public rituals:

- Required regular attendance at a religious service with other people (such as going to church or a synagogue on a certain day of the week);
- Initiation ceremonies that cannot be performed by oneself (such as Christian baptism); and
- Reciting spiritual oaths, creeds, or devotions in public (such as the Apostle's Creed).

PREFERRED PRACTICE #12: TWO IS TO BE A RELIGION THAT DEFIES BEING ORGANIZED INTO A SINGLE ENTITY OR INTO TWO LARGE ENTITIES.

The *Two* religion is not intended to ever be largely organized because an organization can be too easily taken over by special interests or by charismatic personalities. Any special interest group or any particular person must not dominate *Two*.

Spiritual discoveries could, of course, be disseminated faster if the religion were largely organized. Organizing the religion would also allow it to expand more quickly. Wait a minute! Why should we be in a hurry? There is no reason to strive to quickly make this religion a common story. When a person is ready, the religion will be there. The spiritual discoveries of the religion will thereby proceed more slowly; there will be more time to savor each triumph. Each discovery can be experienced thousands of times, each time it is passed on from one person to another. Let the rest of the world's enterprises whirl at any pace they choose; let this religion proceed slowly, beautifully, calmly, one person at a time.

A Simple Prayer Useful for All Occasions

Listen,
Feel:

The Two Sources
are nestled in
among this beauty

celebrating
our blended songs.

©

Appendix #1 The original text for Chapter 1

The United States of America Declaration of Independence

JULY 4, 1776
THE UNANIMOUS DECLARATION OF THE
THIRTEEN UNITED STATES OF AMERICA

When in the course of human events, it becomes
necessary for one people to dissolve the political bands
which have connected them with another, and to
assume among the powers of the earth, the separate and
equal station to which the laws of Nature and of
Nature's God entitle them, a decent respect to the opin-
ions of mankind requires that they should declare the
causes which impel them to the separation.

We hold these truths to be self-evident, that all men
are created equal, that they are endowed by their Creator
with certain unalienable rights, that among these are life,
liberty and the pursuit of happiness. That to secure these
rights, governments are instituted among men, deriving
their just powers from the consent of the governed, That
whenever any form of government becomes destructive

of these ends, it is the right of the people to alter or to abolish it, and to institute new government, laying its foundation on such principles and organizing its powers in such form, as to them shall seem most likely to effect their safety and happiness. Prudence, indeed, will dictate that governments long established should not be changed for light and transient causes; and accordingly all experience hath shown, that mankind are more disposed to suffer, while evils are sufferable, than to right themselves by abolishing the forms to which they are accustomed. But when a long train of abuses and usurpations, pursuing invariably the same object evinces a design to reduce them under absolute despotism, it is their right, it is their duty, to throw off such government, and to provide new guards for their future security. Such has been the patient sufferance of these Colonies; and such is now the necessity which constrains them to alter their former systems of government. The history of the present King of Great Britain is a history of repeated injuries and usurpations, all having in direct object the establishment of an absolute tyranny over these States. To prove this, let facts be submitted to a candid world.

He has refused his assent to laws, the most wholesome and necessary for the public good. He has forbidden his Governors to pass laws of immediate and pressing importance, unless suspended in their operation till his

Assent should be obtained; and when so suspended, he has utterly neglected to attend to them.

He has refused to pass other Laws for the accommodation of large districts of people, unless those people would relinquish the right of representation in the legislature, a right inestimable to them and formidable to tyrants only.

He has called together legislative bodies at places unusual, uncomfortable, and distant from the depository of their public records, for the sole purpose of fatiguing them into compliance with his measures.

He has dissolved Representative Houses repeatedly, for opposing with manly firmness his invasions on the rights of the people.

He has refused for a long time, after such dissolutions, to cause others to be elected; whereby the legislative powers, incapable of annihilation, have returned to the people at large for their exercise; the State remaining in the mean time exposed to all the dangers of invasion from without, and convulsions within.

He has endeavored to prevent the population of these States; for that purpose obstructing the laws for naturalization of foreigners; refusing to pass others to encourage their migration hither, and raising the conditions of new appropriations of lands.

He has obstructed the administration of justice, by refusing his assent to laws for establishing judiciary powers.

He has made judges dependent on his will alone, for the tenure of their offices, and the amount and payment of their salaries.

He has erected a multitude of new offices, and sent hither swarms of officers to harass our people, and eat out their substance.

He has kept among us, in times of peace, standing armies without the Consent of our legislature.

He has affected to render the military independent of and superior to the civil power.

He has combined with others to subject us to a jurisdiction foreign to our constitution, and unacknowledged by our laws; giving his assent to their acts of pretended legislation:

For quartering large bodies of armed troops among us:

For protecting them, by a mock trial, from punishment for any Murders which they should commit on the inhabitants of these States:

For cutting off our trade with all parts of the world:

For imposing taxes on us without our consent:

For depriving us in many cases, of the benefits of trial by jury:

For transporting us beyond seas to be tried for pretended offenses:

For abolishing the free system of English laws in a neighboring province, establishing therein an arbitrary government, and enlarging its boundaries so as to render it at once an example and fit instrument for introducing the same absolute rule into these colonies:

For taking away our charters, abolishing our most valuable laws, and altering fundamentally the forms of our governments:

For suspending our own legislature, and declaring themselves invested with power to legislate for us in all cases whatsoever.

He has abdicated government here, by declaring us out of his protection and waging war against us.

He has plundered our seas, ravaged our coasts, burnt our towns, and destroyed the lives of our people.

He is at this time transporting large armies of foreign mercenaries to complete the works of death, desolation and tyranny, already begun with circumstances of cruelty and perfidy scarcely paralleled in the most barbarous ages, and totally unworthy the head of a civilized nation.

He has constrained our fellow citizens taken captive on the high seas to bear arms against their country, to become the executioners of their friends and brethren, or to fall themselves by their hands.

He has excited domestic insurrections amongst us, and has endeavored to bring on the inhabitants of our frontiers, the merciless Indian Savages, whose known rule of warfare, is an undistinguished destruction of all ages, sexes and conditions.

In every stage of these oppressions we have petitioned for redress in the most humble terms: Our repeated petitions have been answered only by repeated injury. A prince, whole character is thus marked by every act which may define a tyrant, is unfit to be the ruler of a free people.

Nor have we been wanting in attention to our British brethren. We have warned them from time to time of attempts by their legislature to extend an unwarrantable jurisdiction over us. We have reminded them of the circumstances of our emigration and settlement here. We have appealed to their native justice and magnanimity, and we have conjured them by the ties of our common kindred to disavow these usurpations, which, would inevitably interrupt our connections and correspondence. They too have been deaf to the voice of justice and of consanguinity. We must, therefore, acquiesce in the necessity, which denounces our separation, and hold them, as we hold the rest of mankind, enemies in war, in peace friends.

We, therefore, the Representatives of the United States of America, in General Congress, Assembled, appealing to the Supreme Judge of the world for the rectitude of our intentions, do, in the name, and by authority of the good people of these Colonies, solemnly publish and declare, That these United Colonies are, and of right ought to be Free and Independent States; that they are absolved from all allegiance to the British Crown, and that all political connection between them and the State of Great Britain, is and ought to be totally dissolved; and that as free and independent States, they have full power to levy war, conclude peace, contract alliances, establish commerce, and to do all other acts and things which independent States may of right do. And for the support of this Declaration, with a firm reliance on the protection of Divine Providence, we mutually pledge to each other our lives, our fortunes and our sacred honor.

Appendix #2 *The original text for Chapter 2*

The Sixth Ennead, Ninth Tractate: On the Good, or the One From THE SIX ENNEADS by Plotinus, 205-270 CE translated by Stephen MacKenna and B. S. Page

1. It is in virtue of unity that beings are beings.

This is equally true of things whose existence is primal and of all that are in any degree to be numbered among beings. What could exist at all except as one thing? Deprived of unity, a thing ceases to be what it is called: no army unless as a unity: a chorus, a flock, must be one thing. Even house and ship demand unity, one house, one ship; unity gone, neither remains thus even continuous magnitudes could not exist without an inherent unity; break them apart and their very being is altered in the measure of the breach of unity.

Take plant and animal; the material form stands a unity; fallen from that into a litter of fragments, the things have lost their being; what was is no longer there; it is replaced by quite other things-as many others, precisely, as possess unity. Health, similarly, is the condition of a body acting as a co-ordinate unity. Beauty appears when limbs and features are controlled by this principle, unity. Moral excellence is of a soul acting as a concordant total, brought to unity. Come thus to soul-which brings all to unity, making, molding, shaping, ranging to order-there is a temptation to say "Soul is the bestower of unity; soul therefore is the unity." But soul bestows other characteristics upon material things and yet remains distinct from its gift: shape, Ideal-Form and the rest are all distinct from the giving soul; so, clearly, with this gift of unity; soul to make things unities looks out upon the unity just as it makes man by looking upon Man, realizing in the man the unity belonging to Man. Anything that can be described as a unity is so in the precise degree in which it holds a characteristic being; the less or more the degree of the being, the less or more the unity. Soul, while distinct from unity's very self, is a thing of the greater unity in proportion as it is of the greater, the authentic, being. Absolute unity it is not: it is soul and one soul, the unity in some sense a concomitant; there are two things, soul and soul's unity as there is body with body's unity. The looser aggregates, such as a choir, are furthest from unity, the more compact are the nearer; soul is nearer yet but still a participant.

Is soul to be identified with unity on the ground that unless it were one thing it could not be soul? No; unity is equally necessary to every other thing, yet unity stands distinct from them; body and unity are not identical; body, too; is still a participant. Besides, the soul, even the collective soul for all its absence of part, is a manifold: it has diverse powers-reasoning, desiring, perceiving-all held together by this chain of unity. Itself a unity, soul confers unity, but also accepts it.

2. It may be suggested that, while in the unities of the partial order the essence and the unity are distinct, yet in collective existence, in Real Being, they are identical, so that when we have grasped Being we hold unity; Real Being would coincide with Unity.

Thus, taking the Intellectual-Principle as Essential Being, that principle and the Unity Absolute would be at once Primal Being and Pure Unity, purveying, accordingly, to the rest of things something of Being and something, in proportion, of the unity which is itself. There is nothing with which the unity would be more plausibly identified than with Being; either it is Being as a given man is man or it will correspond to the Number which rules in the realm of the particular; it will be a number applying to a certain unique thing as the number two applies to others. Now if Number is a thing among things, then clearly so this unity must be; we would have to discover that thing of things it is. If Number is not a thing but an operation of the mind moving out to reckon, then the unity will not be a thing.

We found that anything losing unity loses its being; we are therefore obliged to enquire whether the unity in particulars is identical with the being, and unity absolute identical with collective being. Now the being of the particular is a manifold; unity cannot be a manifold; there must therefore be a distinction between Being and Unity. Thus a man is at once a reasoning living being and a total of parts; his variety is held together by his unity; man therefore and unity are different-man a thing of parts against unity partless. Much more must Collective Being, as container of all existence, be a manifold and therefore distinct from the unity in which it is but participant. Again, Collective Being contains life and intelligence-it is no dead thing-and so, once more, is a manifold. If Being is identical with Intellectual-Principle, even at that it is a manifold; all the more so when count is taken of the Ideal Forms in it; for the Idea, particular or collective, is, after all, a numerable agglomeration whose unity is that of a cosmos. Above all, unity is The First: but Intellectual-Principle, Ideas and Being, cannot be so; for any member of the realm of Forms is an aggregation, a compound, and therefore-since components must precede their compound-is a later. Other considerations

also go to show that the Intellectual-Principle cannot be
the First. Intellect must be above the Intellectual Act: at
least in its higher phase, that not concerned with the
outer universe, it must be intent upon its Prior; its
introversion is a conversion upon the Principle.
Considered as at once Thinker and Object of its
Thought, it is dual, not simplex, not The Unity:
considered as looking beyond itself, it must look to a
better, to a prior: looking simultaneously upon itself and
upon its Transcendent, it is, once more, not a First. There
is no other way of stating Intellectual-Principle than as
that which, holding itself in the presence of The Good
and First and looking towards That, is self-present also,
self-knowing and Knowing itself as All-Being: thus
manifold, it is far from being The Unity. In sum: The
Unity cannot be the total of beings, for so its oneness is
annulled; it cannot be the Intellectual-Principle, for so it
would be that total which the Intellectual-Principle is;
nor is it Being, for Being is the manifold of things.

3. What then must The Unity be, what nature is left
for it?

No wonder that to state it is not easy; even Being and
Form are not easy, though we have a way, an approach
through the Ideas. The soul or mind reaching towards
the formless finds itself incompetent to grasp where
nothing bounds it or to take impression where the
impinging reality is diffuse; in sheer dread of holding to

nothingness, it slips away. The state is painful; often it seeks relief by retreating from all this vagueness to the region of sense, there to rest as on solid ground, just as the sight distressed by the minute rests with pleasure on the bold.

Soul must see in its own way; this is by coalescence, unification; but in seeking thus to know the Unity it is prevented by that very unification from recognizing that it has found; it cannot distinguish itself from the object of this intuition. Nonetheless, this is our one resource if our philosophy is to give us knowledge of The Unity.

We are in search of unity; we are to come to know the principle of all, the Good and First; therefore we may not stand away from the realm of Firsts and lie prostrate among the lasts: we must strike for those Firsts, rising from things of sense which are the lasts. Cleared of all evil in our intention towards The Good, we must ascend to the Principle within ourselves; from many, we must become one; only so do we attain to knowledge of that which is Principle and Unity. We shape ourselves into Intellectual-Principle; we make over our soul in trust to Intellectual-Principle and set it firmly in That; thus what That sees the soul will waken to see; it is through the Intellectual-Principle that we have this vision of The Unity; it must be our care to bring over nothing whatever from sense, to allow nothing even of soul to enter into Intellectual-Principle: with Intellect pure, and with the summit of Intellect, we are to see the All-Pure.

If quester has the impression of extension or shape or mass attaching to That Nature he has not been led by Intellectual-Principle which is not of the order to see such things; the activity has been of sense and of the judgement following upon sense: only Intellectual-Principle can inform us of the things of its scope; its competence is upon its priors, its content and its issue: but even its content is outside of sense; and still purer, still less touched by multiplicity, are its priors, or rather its Prior. The Unity, then, is not Intellectual-Principle but something higher still: Intellectual-Principle is still a being but that First is no being but precedent to all Being; it cannot be a being, for a being has what we may call the shape of its reality but The Unity is without shape, even shape Intellectual. Generative of all, The Unity is none of all; neither thing nor quantity nor quality nor intellect nor soul; not in motion, not at rest, not in place, not in time: it is the self-defined, unique in form or, better, formless, existing before Form was, or Movement or Rest, all of which are attachments of Being and make Being the manifold it is. But how, if not in movement, can it be otherwise than at rest? The answer is that movement and rest are states pertaining to Being, which necessarily has one or the other or both. Besides, anything at rest must be so in virtue of Rest as something distinct: Unity at rest becomes the ground of an attribute and at once ceases to be a simplex.

Note, similarly, that, when we speak of this First as Cause, we are affirming something happening not to it but to us, the fact that we take from this Self-Enclosed: strictly we should put neither a This nor a That to it; we hover, as it were, about it, seeking the statement of an experience of our own, sometimes nearing this Reality, sometimes baffled by the enigma in which it dwells.

4. The main part of the difficulty is that awareness of this Principle comes neither by knowing nor by the Intellection that discovers the Intellectual Beings but by a presence overpassing all knowledge.

In knowing, soul or mind abandons its unity; it cannot remain a simplex: knowing is taking account of things; that accounting is multiple; the mind, thus plunging into number and multiplicity, departs from unity. Our way then takes us beyond knowing; there may be no wandering from unity; knowing and knowable must all be left aside; every object of thought, even the highest, we must pass by, for all that is good is later than This and derives from This as from the sun all the light of the day. "Not to be told; not to be written": in our writing and telling we are but urging towards it: out of discussion we call to vision: to those desiring to see, we point the path; our teaching is of the road and the travelling; the seeing must be the very act of one that has made this choice.

There are those that have not attained to see. The soul has not come to know the splendor There; it has not felt and clutched to itself that love-passion of vision known to lover come to rest where he loves. Or struck perhaps by that authentic light, all the soul lit by the nearness gained, we have gone weighted from beneath; the vision is frustrate; we should go without burden and we go carrying that which can but keep us back; we are not yet made over into unity. From none is that Principle absent and yet from all: present, it remains absent save to those fit to receive, disciplined into some accordance, able to touch it closely by their likeness and by that kindred power within themselves through which, remaining as it was when it came to them from the Supreme, they are enabled to see in so far as God may at all be seen. Failure to attain may be due to such impediment or to lack of the guiding thought that establishes trust; impediment we must charge against ourselves and strive by entire renunciation to become emancipate; where there is distrust for lack of convincing reason, further considerations may be applied:

5. Those to whom existence comes about by chance and automatic action and is held together by material forces have drifted far from God and from the concept of unity; we are not here addressing them but only such as accept another nature than body and have some conception of soul.

Soul must be sounded to the depths, understood as an emanation from Intellectual-Principle and as holding its value by a Reason-Principle thence infused. Next this Intellect must be apprehended, an Intellect other than the reasoning faculty known as the rational principle; with reasoning we are already in the region of separation and movement: our sciences are Reason-Principles lodged in soul or mind, having manifestly acquired their character by the presence in the soul of Intellectual-Principle, source of all knowing.

Thus we come to see Intellectual-Principle almost as an object of sense: the Intellectual Cosmos is perceptible as standing above soul, father to soul: we know Intellectual-Principle as the motionless, not subject to change, containing, we must think, all things; a multiple but at once indivisible and comporting difference. It is not discriminate as are the Reason-Principles, which can in fact be known one by one: yet its content is not a confusion; every item stands forth distinctly, just as in a science the entire content holds as an indivisible and yet each item is a self-standing verity.

Now a plurality thus concentrated like the Intellectual Cosmos is close upon The First-and reason certifies its existence as surely as that of soul-yet, though of higher sovereignty than soul, it is not The First since it is not a unity, not simplex as unity, principle over all multiplicity, must be. Before it there is That which must transcend the noblest of the things of Being: there must be a prior to this Principle which aiming towards unity is yet not unity but a thing in unity's likeness. From this highest it is not sundered; it too is self-present: so close to the unity, it cannot be articulated: and yet it is a principle which in some measure has dared secession.

That awesome Prior, The Unity, is not a being, for so its unity would be vested in something else: strictly no name is apt to it, but since name it we must there is a certain rough fitness in designating it as unity with the understanding that it is not the unity of some other thing. Thus it eludes our knowledge, so that the nearer approach to it is through its offspring, Being: we know it as cause of existence to Intellectual-Principle, as fount of all that is best, as the efficacy which, self-perduring and undiminishing, generates all beings and is not to be counted among these its derivatives, to all of which it must be prior.

This we can but name The Unity, indicating it to each other by a designation that points to the concept of its partlessness while we are in reality striving to bring our own minds to unity. We are not to think of such unity and partlessness as belong to point or monad; the veritable unity is the source of all such quantity which could not exist unless first there existed Being and Being's Prior: we are not, then, to think in the order of point and monad but to use these-in their rejection of magnitude and partition-as symbols for the higher concept.

6. In what sense, then, do we assert this Unity, and how is it to be adjusted to our mental processes?

Its oneness must not be entitled to that of monad and point: for these the mind abstracts extension and numerical quantity and rests upon the very minutest possible, ending no doubt in the partless but still in something that began as a partible and is always lodged in something other than itself. The Unity was never in any other and never belonged to the partible: nor is its impartibility that of extreme minuteness; on the contrary it is great beyond anything, great not in extension but in power, sizeless by its very greatness as even its immediate sequents are impartible not in mass but in might. We must therefore take the Unity as infinite not in measureless extension or numerable quantity but in fathomless depths of power.

Think of The One as Mind or as God, you think too meanly; use all the resources of understanding to conceive this Unity and, again, it is more authentically one than God, even though you reach for God's unity beyond the unity the most perfect you can conceive. For This is utterly a self-existent, with no concomitant whatever. This self-sufficing is the essence of its unity. Something there must be supremely adequate, autonomous, all-transcending, most utterly without need.

Any manifold, anything beneath The Unity, is dependent; combined from various constituents, its essential nature goes in need of unity; but unity cannot

need itself; it stands unity accomplished. Again, a manifold depends upon all its factors; and furthermore each
of those factors in turn-as necessarily inbound with the
rest and not self-standing-sets up a similar need both to
its associates and to the total so constituted.

The sovranly self-sufficing principle will be Unity-
Absolute, for only in this Unity is there a nature above all
need, whether within itself or in regard to the rest of
things. Unity seeks nothing towards its being or its well-
being or its safehold upon existence; cause to all, how can
it acquire its character outside of itself or know any good
outside? The good of its being can be no borrowing: This
is The Good. Nor has it station; it needs no standing
ground as if inadequate to its own sustaining; what calls
for such underpropping is the soulless, some material
mass that must be based or fall. This is base to all, cause
of universal existence and of ordered station. All that
demands place is in need; a First cannot go in need of its
sequents: all need is effort towards a first principle; the
First, principle to all, must be utterly without need. If the
Unity be seeking, it must inevitably be seeking to be
something other than itself; it is seeking its own
destroyer. Whatever may be said to be in need of a good
is needing a preserver; nothing can be a good to The
Unity, therefore.

Neither can it have will to anything; it is a Beyond-
Good, not even to itself a good but to such beings only
as may be of quality to have part with it. Nor has it

Intellection; that would comport diversity: nor movement; it is prior to Movement as to Intellection. To
what could its Intellection be directed? To itself? But
that would imply a previous ignorance; it would be
dependent upon that Intellection in order to knowledge
of itself; but it is the self-sufficing. Yet this absence of
self-knowing does not comport ignorance; ignorance is
of something outside-a knower ignorant of a know-
able-but in the Solitary there is neither knowing nor
anything unknown. Unity, self-present, it has no need
of self-intellection: indeed this "self-presence" were
better left out, the more surely to preserve the unity; we
must eliminate all knowing and all association, all intellection whether internal or external. It is not to be
though of as having but as being Intellection;
Intellection does not itself perform the intellective act
but is the cause of the act in something else, and cause
is not to be identified with caused: most assuredly the
cause of all is not a thing within that all. This Principle
is not, therefore, to be identified with the good of
which it is the source; it is good in the unique mode of
being The Good above all that is good.

7. If the mind reels before something thus alien to all
we know, we must take our stand on the things of this
realm and strive thence to see.

But, in the looking, beware of throwing outward; this
Principle does not lie away somewhere leaving the rest

void; to those of power to reach, it is present; to the inapt, absent. In our daily affairs we cannot hold an object in mind if we have given ourselves elsewhere, occupied upon some other matter; that very thing must be before us to be truly the object of observation. So here also; preoccupied by the impress of something else, we are withheld under that pressure from becoming aware of The Unity; a mind gripped and fastened by some definite thing cannot take the print of the very contrary. As Matter, it is agreed, must be void of quality in order to accept the types of the universe, so and much more must the soul be kept formless if there is to be no infixed impediment to prevent it being brimmed and lit by the Primal Principle. In sum, we must withdraw from all the extern, pointed wholly inwards; no leaning to the outer; the total of things ignored, first in their relation to us and later in the very idea; the self put out of mind in the contemplation of the Supreme; all the commerce so closely There that, if report were possible, one might become to others reporter of that communion. Such converse, we may suppose, was that of Minos, thence known as the Familiar of Zeus; and in that memory he established the laws which report it, enlarged to that task by his vision There. Some, on the other hand, there will be to disdain such citizen service, choosing to remain in the higher: these will be those that have seen much.

God-we read-is outside of none, present unperceived to all; we break away from Him, or rather from ourselves; what we turn from we cannot reach; astray ourselves, we cannot go in search of another; a child distraught will not recognize its father; to find ourselves is to know our source.

8. Every soul that knows its history is aware, also, that its movement, unthwarted, is not that of an outgoing line; its natural course may be likened to that in which a circle turns not upon some external but on its own center, the point to which it owes its rise.

The soul's movement will be about its source; to this it will hold, poised intent towards that unity to which all souls should move and the divine souls always move, divine in virtue of that movement; for to be a god is to be integral with the Supreme; what stands away is man still multiple, or beast. Is then this "center" of our souls the Principle for which we are seeking?

We must look yet further: we must admit a Principle in which all these centers coincide: it will be a center by analogy with the center of the circle we know. This is the message that we have been looking for. A competition of a cyclical loop. An acknowledged and proper place to begin. The soul is not a circle in the sense of the geometric figure but in that it at once contains the Primal Nature [as center] and is contained by it [as circumference], that it owes its origin to such a center and still more that the soul, uncontaminated, is a self-contained entity.

In our present state-part of our being weighed down by the body, as one might have the feet under water with all the rest untouched-we bear ourselves aloft by that intact part and, in that, hold through our own center to the center of all the centers, just as the centers of the great circles of a sphere coincide with that of the sphere to which all belong. Thus we are secure. If these circles were material and not spiritual, the link with the centers would be local; they would lie round it where it lay at some distant point: since the souls are of the Intellectual, and the Supreme still loftier, we understand that contact is otherwise procured, that is by those powers which connect Intellectual agent with Intellectual Object; this all the more, since the Intellect grasps the Intellectual object by the way of similarity, identity, in the sure link of kindred. Material mass cannot blend into other material mass: unbodied beings are not under this bodily limitation; their separation is solely that of otherness, of differentiation; in the absence of otherness, it is similars mutually present.

Thus the Supreme as containing no otherness is ever present with us; we with it when we put otherness away. It is not that the Supreme reaches out to us seeking our communion: we reach towards the Supreme; it is we that become present. We are always before it: but we do not always look: thus a choir, singing set in due order about the conductor, may turn away from that center to which all should attend: let it but face aright and it sings with beauty, present effectively. We are ever before the Supreme-cut off is utter dissolution; we can no longer be-but we do not always attend: when we look, our Term is attained; this is rest; this is the end of singing ill; effectively before Him, we lift a choral song full of God.

9. In this choiring, the soul looks upon the wellspring of Life, wellspring also of Intellect, beginning of Being, fount of Good, root of Soul. It is not that these are poured out from the Supreme lessening it as if it were a thing of mass.

At that the emanants would be perishable; but they are eternal; they spring from an eternal principle, which produces them not by its fragmentation but in virtue of its intact identity: therefore they too hold firm; so long as the sun shines, so long there will be light. We have not been cut away; we are not separate, what though the body-nature has closed about us to press us to itself; we breathe and hold our ground because the Supreme does not give and pass but gives on for ever, so long as it remains what it is.

Our being is the fuller for our turning Thither; this is our prosperity; to hold aloof is loneliness and lessening. Here is the soul's peace, outside of evil, refuge taken in the place clean of wrong; here it has its Act, its true knowing; here it is immune. Here is living, the true; that of to-day, all living apart from Him, is but a shadow, a mimicry. Life in the Supreme is the native activity of Intellect; in virtue of that converse it brings forth gods, brings forth beauty, brings forth righteousness, brings forth all moral good; for of all these the soul is pregnant when it has been filled with God. This state is its first and its final, because from God it comes, its good lies There, and, once turned to God again, it is what it was. Life here, with the things of earth, is a sinking, a defeat, a failing of the wing.

That our good is There is shown by the very love inborn with the soul; hence the constant linking of the Love-God with the Psyches in story and picture; the soul, other than God but sprung of Him, must needs love. So long as it is There, it holds the heavenly love; here its love is the baser; There the soul is Aphrodite of the heavens; here, turned harlot, Aphrodite of the public ways: yet the soul is always an Aphrodite. This is the intention of the myth which tells of Aphrodite's birth and Eros born with her.

The soul in its nature loves God and longs to be at one with Him in the noble love of a daughter for a noble father; but coming to human birth and lured by the courtships of this sphere, she takes up with another love, a mortal, leaves her father and falls. But one day coming to hate her shame, she puts away the evil of earth, once more seeks the father, and finds her peace. Those to whom all this experience is strange may understand by way of our earthly longings and the joy we have in winning to what we most desire-remembering always that here what we love is perishable, hurtful, that our loving is of mimicries and turns awry because all was a mistake, our good was not here, this was not what we sought; There only is our veritable love and There we may hold it and be with it, possess it in its verity no longer submerged in alien flesh. Any that have seen know what I have in mind: the soul takes another life as it approaches God; thus restored it feels that the dispenser of true life is There to see, that now we have nothing to look for but, far otherwise, that we must put aside all else and rest in This alone, This become, This alone, all the earthly environment done away, in haste to be free, impatient of any bond holding us to the baser, so that with our being entire we may cling about This, no part in us remaining but through it we have touch with God.

Thus we have all the vision that may be of Him and of ourselves; but it is of a self-wrought to splendor, brimmed with the Intellectual light, become that very light, pure, buoyant, unburdened, raised to Godhood or, better, knowing its Godhood, all aflame then-but crushed out once more if it should take up the discarded burden.

10. But how comes the soul not to keep that ground?
Because it has not yet escaped wholly: but there will be the time of vision unbroken, the self hindered no longer by any hindrance of body. Not that those hindrances beset that in us which has veritably seen; it is

the other phase of the soul that suffers and that only when we withdraw from vision and take to knowing by proof, by evidence, by the reasoning processes of the mental habit. Such logic is not to be confounded with that act of ours in the vision; it is not our reason that has seen; it is something greater than reason, reason's Prior, as far above reason as the very object of that thought must be.

In our self-seeing There, the self is seen as belonging to that order, or rather we are merged into that self in us which has the quality of that order. It is a knowing of the self restored to its purity. No doubt we should not speak of seeing; but we cannot help talking in dualities, seen and seer, instead of, boldly, the achievement of unity. In this seeing, we neither hold an object nor trace distinction; there is no two. The man is changed, no longer himself nor self-belonging; he is merged with the Supreme, sunken into it, one with it: center coincides with center, for on this higher plane things that touch at all are one; only in separation is there duality; by our holding away, the Supreme is set outside. This is why the vision baffles telling; we cannot detach the Supreme to state it; if we have seen something thus detached we have failed of the Supreme which is to be known only as one with ourselves.

11. This is the purport of that rule of our Mysteries: Nothing Divulged to the Uninitiated: the Supreme is

not to be made a common story, the holy things may not be uncovered to the stranger, to any that has not himself attained to see.

There were not two; beholder was one with beheld; it was not a vision compassed but a unity apprehended. The man formed by this mingling with the Supreme must-if he only remember-carry its image impressed upon him: he is become the Unity, nothing within him or without inducing any diversity; no movement now, no passion, no outlooking desire, once this ascent is achieved; reasoning is in abeyance and all Intellection and even, to dare the word, the very self; caught away, filled with God, he has in perfect stillness attained isolation; all the being calmed, he turns neither to this side nor to that, not even inwards to himself; utterly resting he has become very rest. He belongs no longer to the order of the beautiful; he has risen beyond beauty; he has overpassed even the choir of the virtues; he is like one who, having penetrated the inner sanctuary, leaves the temple images behind him-though these become once more first objects of regard when he leaves the holies; for There his converse was not with image, not with trace, but with the very Truth in the view of which all the rest is but of secondary concern.

There, indeed, it was scarcely vision, unless of a mode unknown; it was a going forth from the self, a simplifying, a renunciation, a reach towards contact and at the same time a repose, a meditation towards adjustment.

This is the only seeing of what lies within the holies: to look otherwise is to fail.

Things here are signs; they show therefore to the wiser teachers how the supreme God is known; the instructed priest reading the sign may enter the holy place and make real the vision of the inaccessible. Even those that have never found entry must admit the existence of that invisible; they will know their source and Principle since by principle they see principle and are linked with it, by like they have contact with like and so they grasp all of the divine that lies within the scope of mind. Until the seeing comes they are still craving..something, that which only the vision can give; this Term, attained only by those that have overpassed all, is the All-Transcending. It is not in the soul's nature to touch utter nothingness; the lowest descent is into evil and, so far, into non-being: but to utter nothing, never. When the soul begins again to mount, it comes not to something alien but to its very self; thus detached, it is not in nothingness but in itself; self-gathered it is no longer in the order of being; it is in the Supreme.

There is thus a converse in virtue of which the essential man outgrows Being, becomes identical with the Transcendent of Being. The self thus lifted, we are in the likeness of the Supreme: if from that heightened self we pass still higher-image to archetype-we have won the Term of all our journeying. Fallen back again, we awaken the virtue within until we know ourselves all order once more; once more we are lightened of the burden and move by virtue towards Intellectual-Principle and through the Wisdom in That to the Supreme.

This is the life of gods and of the godlike and blessed among men, liberation from the alien that besets us here, a life taking no pleasure in the things of earth, the passing of solitary to solitary.

Appendix #3 *The original text for Chapter 3*

25
How is it with this love,
I see your world and not you?

77
For years, copying other people, I tried to know myself.
From within, I couldn't decide what to do.
Unable to see, I heard my name being called
Then I walked outside.

158
Out beyond ideas or wrongdoing and rightdoing,
There is a field. I'll meet you there.

511

The clear bead at the center changes everything.
There are no edges to my loving now.

I've heard it said there's a window that opens
From one mind to another,

But if there's no wall, there's no need
For fitting the window, or the latch.

Who Says Words With My Mouth

All day I think about it, then at night I say it.
Where did I come from, and what am I suppose to be
doing?
I have no idea.
My soul is from elsewhere, I'm sure of that,
And I intend to end up there.

This drunkenness began in some other tavern.
When I get back around to that place,
I'll be completely sober. Meanwhile,
I'm like a bird from another continent, sitting in this
aviary.
The day is coming when I fly off,
But who is it now in my ear, who hears my voice?
Who says words with my mouth?

Who looks out with my eyes? What is the soul?
I cannot stop asking.

If I could taste on sip of an answer,
I could break out of this prison for drunks.
I didn't come here of my own accord, and I can't leave
that way.
Let whoever brought me here take me back.

This poetry, I never know what I'm going to say.
I don't plan it.
When I'm outside the saying of it,
I get very quiet and rarely speak at all.

Answers from the Elements
A whole afternoon field inside me from one stem or
reed.
The messenger comes running toward me, irritated:
Why be so hard to find?

Last night I asked the Moon, my one question
for the visible world, Where is God?
The moon says, *I am dust stirred up
when he passed by.* The sun, *My face is pale yellow
from just now seeing him.* Water: *I slide on my head and face
Like a snake, from a spell he said.* Fire: *His lightning.
I want to be that restless.* Wind, why so light?
I would burn if I had a choice. Earth, quiet
And thoughtful? *Inside me I have a garden
and an underground spring.*

This world hurts my head with its answers,
Wine filling my hand, now my glass.
If I could wake completely, I would say without speak-
ing
Why I'm ashamed of using words.

The Bottle Is Corked

The rock splits open like wings beat
air, wanting. Campfire gives in to rain,
but I can't go to sleep, or be patient.

Part of me wants to eat the stones
and hold you back when you're leaving,
till your good laughing turns bitter and wrong.

I worry I won't have someone to talk to, and breathe
with.
Don't you understand I'm some kind of food for you?
I'm a place where you can work.

The bottle is corked and sitting on the table.
Someone comes in and sees me without you
and puts his hand on my head like I'm a child.
This is so difficult.

1246

The minute I heard my first love story
I started looking for you, not knowing
how blind that was.

Lovers don't finally meet somewhere,
They're in each other all along.

1242
During the day I was singing with you.
At night we slept in the same bed.
I wasn't conscious day or night.
I thought I knew who I was,
But I was you.

Unmarked Boxes
Don't grieve. Anything you lose come round
In another form. The child weaned from mother's milk
now drinks wine and honey mixed.

God's joy moves from unmarked box to unmarked box,
From cell to cell. As rainwater, down into flowerbed,
as roses, up from ground.
Now it looks like a plate of rice and fish,
now a cliff covered with vines,
now a horse being saddled.
It hides within these,
till one day, it cracks them open.

Part of the self leaves the body when we sleep
And changes shape. You might say, "Last night
I was a cypress tree, a small bed of tulips,
a field of grapevines." The phantasm goes away.

You're back in the room.
I don't want to make any one fearful.
Hear what's behind what I say.

Fa'ilatun fa'ilatun fa'ilatun fa'ilat.
There's the light gold of wheat in the sun
and the gold of bread made from the whet.
I have neither. I'm only talking about them,

as a town in the desert looks up
at stars on a clear night.

Be Melting Snow
Totally conscious, and apropos of nothing, he comes to
see me.
Is someone here? I ask.
The moon. The full moon is inside your house.

My friends and I go running out into the street.
I'm in here, comes a voice from the house, but we aren't
listening.
We're looking up at the sky.
My pet nightingale sobs like a drunk in the garden.
Ringdoves scatter with small cries, *Where, Where.*
It's midnight. The whole neighborhood is up and out in
the street
thinking, *The cat-burglar has come back.*
The actual thief is there too, saying out loud,

Yes, the cat-burglar is somewhere in this crowd.
No one pays attention.

Lo, I am with you always, means when you look for God,
God is in the look of your eyes,
in the thought of looking, nearer to you than your self,
or things that have happened to you.
There's no need to go outside.
Be melting snow.
Wash yourself of yourself.

A white flower grows in the quietness.
Let your tongue become that flower.

1245
Since we've seen each other, a game goes on.
Secretly I move, and you respond.
You're winning, you think it's funny.

But look up from the board now, look how
I've brought in furniture to this invisible place,
so we can live here.

After Being in Love, the Next Responsibility
Turn me like a waterwheel turning a millstone.
Plenty of water, Living Water.
Keep me in one place and scatter the love.

Leaf moves in a wind, straw drawn toward amber,
all parts of the world are in love,
but they do not tell their secrets: Cows grazing
on a sacramental table, ants whispering in Solomon's ear.
Mountains mumbling an echo. Sky calm.
If the sun were not in love, he would have no brightness
the side of the hill no grass on it.
The ocean would come to rest somewhere.
Be a lover as they are, that you come to know
your Beloved. Be faithful that you may know
Faith. The other parts of the universe did not accept
the next responsibility of love as you can.
They were afraid they might make a mistake
with it, the inspired knowing
that springs from being in love.